EXPRESSING YOUR ORIGINALITY IN A WORLD
SUFFOCATING FROM SAMENESS

LARRY RANDOLPH

Cover: Steve Fryer (www.stevefryer.com)

Larry Randolph Ministries
PO Box 682965
Franklin, TN 37068
info@larryrandolph.com

www.larryrandolph.com

ISBN 978-0-615-38356-9
For Worldwide Distribution
Printed in the U.S.A.

Acknowledgements

Many thanks go to Holly Giersch. Your kind yet persistent challenge to clarify my thoughts on various issues has greatly increased the readability of this book. I am also grateful for the skill and patience you exhibited throughout much of the editing process. You are truly God-sent, and your contribution is invaluable.

My heartfelt gratitude also goes to Diana Kay Woods. Your expertise in fine-tuning the final edit of this manuscript is very much appreciated. I am deeply thankful for your creative input and the thoughtful suggestions that you made. Your hard work to push this project forward to completion is beyond the call of duty. You are a great blessing. Thanks to David Sluka for your last-minute help to get this project done.

Also, huge appreciation goes to my wife, Laura, who has demonstrated to me the value of authenticity. Your passion for originality and your unusual ability to see through the many counterfeits and imitations in this world is refreshing. Especially inspiring is your desire to become the unique person you were created to be. You are amazingly original and your life is a remarkable gift from God. Thank you for believing in me and for your encouragement to express myself through writing.

Most importantly, I am deeply grateful to the Creator who is the original artist and the architect of diversity. By observing the vast originality that You display in the universe, I have come into a deeper understanding of Your creative genius. Thank You for placing in my heart a divine dissatisfaction with imitations of life and religion. You have stirred in me an appetite for authenticity that gives me the courage to be myself. For that freedom I am extremely grateful.

Table of Contents

Introduction

One of the most astonishing aspects of human existence is the gift of individuality. Each and every person is a child of intelligent design and reflects the unique artistry of the Creator. This means that our lives were predetermined by God, and our individuality is the outcome of divine intention. In the totality of our being, we are an original work of art, a one-of-a-kind gift to the world.

The problem is that most of us don't appreciate our distinct existence, nor do we believe that we possess a unique life that sets us apart from the other six billion people on Earth today. Even though we were born with an original self, the tragedy is that many of us will live and die as a copy. The Irish writer Oscar Wilde said it best when he wrote:

> "Most people are other people. Their thoughts are someone else's opinion, their lives a mockery, their passions a quotation."

What can we do to counteract the epidemic of sameness that is rampant in much of the world today? How do we find our authentic reality and truly become the extraordinary person we were created to be?

First of all, we must live as original creations with lives like no other. That means we have to resist the temptation to live a copycat existence and break free from the personal constraints that keep us from finding our authentic selves. I know that's easier said than done. But to live a life beyond ordinary, we need to value the importance of being genuine and real. We must dare to be different, and most importantly we must learn to express our God-given individuality without reservation or apology. Quite simply, we must embrace the intelligent design of our remarkable existence.

The Need for Permission

All too often, the person we aspire to be is someone we never become. It's unfortunate, but many people allow their quest for authenticity to be sabotaged by the fear of failure. Imprisoned by self-doubt, they play it safe and are often reluctant to break out of their comfort zone and take a risk. Overwhelmed by feelings of inadequacy, the prospect of living out their destiny is more of a fantasy than a reality.

Considering the consequences of this crippling perception, I spent a great deal of time contemplating the theme of this manuscript. I was deeply aware of the importance of offering straightforward answers that could motivate people to realize their potential. To help them reach their God-given purpose, I knew that I had to present key insights that are uncomplicated, yet powerful in application.

That's when it hit me: People need permission! As most research shows, the need for approval and affirmation is a primal aspect of human nature that's ever-present in our lives. At birth, for example, we had to be firmly persuaded to take our first gulp of air. As toddlers, we were also coaxed into taking our first step and were encouraged to continue walking even though we often fell down. Then after learning to walk and speak, we were taught to ask permission to leave the dinner table and were instructed to raise our hand for permission to speak in school. As we approached adulthood, we were also expected to ask our parents for approval to date and finally for their consent to marry.

In the same way, I believe the power of permission is the driving force behind the discovery of our individual destinies. Because of the positive impact it has on our lives, all of us need the encouragement to become the person we were created to be. Not only do we need permission to embrace our unique existence, but we need encouragement to express that same God-given uniqueness without guilt or shame. We desperately need someone to say it's alright to be authentically different—to be ourselves and to "breathe" the life we were created to breathe. Otherwise, we run the risk of suppressing our distinct personality and living a life that is out of step with our destiny.

The Power of Permission

Recently, while conducting a seminar in North Carolina, I felt prompted to address this issue. During one of the sessions, I spoke to the international group about being authentic and I mentioned some of the key concepts in this book.

Then on the last night, I ended the conference with a bold challenge. I dared everyone in the room to tell me about their hopes and dreams and what they believed they were created to be and do. I assured them that if they would speak out the desires of their hearts, I would, as a spiritual father, give them permission to pursue their passions.

One by one, as they began to declare their hopes and dreams, each person received a verbal affirmation from me, along with a round of applause from the group. One housewife confessed her lifelong passion to be an artist. Another lady talked about her dream to start an orphanage. Some of the businessmen had deep longings for ministry, while several of the pastors had secret desires to work in the marketplace.

Others expressed hidden desires for acting, music, writing, sculpting, pastoring, leading worship and a number of other uncultivated talents and professions. At the end of the meeting, I could see hope on many of their faces and sensed that the affirmation they received would allow them to pursue their wildest dreams.

Thinking I had achieved my goal, I gathered my personal belongings and went upstairs to the hospitality room seeking snacks and coffee. After several minutes of self-indulgence, I noticed that no one had followed me out of the meeting. Then, almost on cue, I heard what sounded like the muffled sounds of laughter and singing drifting up the staircase to the second story. It sounded like a party in full swing.

At that point, several of my friends ran up the stairs to tell me what I had already suspected. The well-ordered meeting had turned into a noisy, joyful celebration that was now out of control. They told me that my wife, Laura, who is normally quite reserved in public, was dancing joyfully around the room. I was further informed that my former assistant, Holly, and several other ladies had formed a wild and jubilant dance circle. "You better come back to the meeting," they said. "The whole place is going bananas."

Overcome with curiosity, I ran downstairs to witness the crazy, chaotic scene that was rapidly unfolding. Much to my surprise, the soundman was playing the piano and a young, stoic Englishman was beating on a set of bongos. I was also shocked to see several of the Korean pastors and businessmen dancing and jumping with enthusiasm, as though they had just won the lottery. Most amusing to me was the Norwegian man who had been detached during much of the seminar but now seemed to be drunk with joy and was laughing uncontrollably. And to top it off, a rather conservative lady surprised us all when she grabbed a microphone and began to rap in perfect rhythm and rhyme.

As long as I live, I will never forget the look of enthusiasm on everyone's face that night. Many of the people were freed from their inhibitions and charged with creative expression. Apparently, my affirmation had produced an atmosphere of expectation, giving each of them hope to become the person they always wanted to be. I knew, of course, that the excitement would subside when they returned to the routine of their daily lives. Even so, I was optimistic that this might be the beginning of a journey to discover their authentic selves—empowering them to live a life beyond ordinary.

Permission Granted!

The riveting scene that night sparked in me a desire to release the power of permission to people who are insecure about expressing their individuality. As I've said, the Creator has given you an extraordinary existence that needs to be recognized and affirmed. You desperately need the permission to be you, even if that means being radically different from everyone else in the world.

Bear in mind, though, that your life will reach maximum impact only to the degree that you're willing to be an original. That's the purpose of this book—to give you permission to discover the person you were always meant to be. I want to encourage you to dare to be yourself and never settle for being an imitation of someone else. You are truly one of a kind and have the potential to live a remarkable life. In fact, your journey to find authentic life begins the moment you find the courage to embrace your own unique destiny.

However, to fully appreciate your God-given uniqueness, it's important to understand the creative genius of the One who made you in His image. As you will see in the first few chapters, the vast range of diversity found in humanity and the universe is not accidental. It is the master plan of a Creator who has breathed distinction into every aspect of His creation. In a marvelous way, that distinction is a gift from God that makes you an exceptional human being.

PART
ONE

*Recognizing the Genius
of God in Creation*

1

Maximum Diversity

"Diversity is the one thing that every living
organism and dust particle in the
universe shares in common."
—Larry Randolph—

Curiosity about life and the universe is God's subtle voice guiding us to Himself.

As a small boy growing up in a ministry family, I found this to be true in every sense of the word. Many were the nights I dragged my blanket onto the grassy field behind our little house, eager to search the heavens for a sign from God. Lying on my back, I would gaze into the starry night for hours at a time, pondering the mysterious workings of the universe.

How could I ever understand such an awesome Creator as God? Who was He? Why did He create me? And what was my reason for being on Earth?

Although I never heard a reply from Heaven, I took great comfort in the breathtaking display of heavenly lights before my eyes. Occasionally, a shimmering star acknowledged my childlike curiosity and would twinkle in synchronization with every heartbeat. And when I needed further affirmation of God's love, shooting stars would often streak across the sky, as if to say that the Creator was out there somewhere watching me from a distance.

Later in the night, after my parents put me to bed, I would continue my contemplation into the early morning. Nestled under the covers and wide awake, I strained my little brain trying to comprehend a God with no beginning or end—a God who created all the stars I had attempted to count earlier that night. When sleep finally overtook my exhausted body, I would drift in and out of mystifying dreams about destiny, life, and eternity.

The Ultimate Artist

Although many decades have come and gone since those early days of childhood, I am no less fascinated by the mystery of God and life. Every now and then, I still go outdoors on a starry night and gaze at the sky, hoping to hear a whisper from Heaven. More than ever before, I am determined to grow in my discovery of God and the meaning of human existence—even if it takes the rest of my life.

However, this quest is not without challenges. It seems the more I learn about the Creator and His unique creation, the less I really understand. Honestly, it feels as though I have climbed part way up an enormous mountain only to discover how far I still have to go. And the closer I get to the summit, the more I stand in awe of a majestic God who patiently awaits my arrival.

> It would take a million eternities to define even one speck of God's creative genius.

Who is this God and how does He relate to His creation?

By my own admission, I may not be the most qualified to answer this question. Perhaps such a daunting task should be addressed by someone with extensive theological training or someone with a longer history with God than myself. Even if I were the most articulate person on Earth, it would still take a million eternities to define even one speck of God's creative genius. That being said, I'm going to give it my best shot.

I have discovered that the Creator is outrageously clever and mysteriously complex. As seen in 1 Timothy 1:17, His existence is without beginning or end, and He lives in a dimension of eternity that has no boundaries of time or space. In mysterious language, Revelation 4:8 describes the Almighty as "He who is, who was, and who is to come."

The same cloud of mystery also surrounds God's character and nature. In fact, the makeup of His personality is so unique that the Hebrew Old Testament uses numerous names and titles to describe His person. Yet when Moses struggled with God's identity in Exodus 3, the God of many names defined Himself with an uncomplicated but profound description that has baffled Bible theologians for centuries. The Lord told the bewildered prophet that His nickname is simply "I Am."

Even more perplexing are other aspects of God's personality that defy human reasoning. With regard to the heart of the Lord, the sum of His benevolence is off the charts. In Psalm 89:24-36, David declares that God's majesty and splendor are boundless and His loving-kindness is everlasting—reaching to all generations. This says to me that His goodness is equal in measure to His sovereignty. My friend Graham Cooke lovingly describes God as "the kindest person I've ever known."

Another amazing facet of God's greatness is His passionate creativity that He poured into humanity in Genesis 2. With every stroke of His brush, the Creator transferred a piece of His creative brilliance to the canvas of human life—making Adam and Eve in His image and likeness. He then breathed into the nostrils of this unique creation and the art took on the life of the artist, becoming a living reflection of the Creator's innermost being. In a stunning display of creative genius, God had fully invested Himself in the parents of a human race that would carry His divine persona and original breath.

The Architect of Diversity

Another astonishing characteristic of God's genius is His diverse creativity displayed in the cosmos. Before the creation of mankind, the Almighty single-handedly masterminded a universe that is extraordinarily unique. As seen in Genesis, He is both the architect and guardian of diversity and set certain laws of nature in motion to safeguard the distinct character of His handiwork.

With respect to God's diversity throughout the universe, the great Albert Einstein provided the following quote in the *Saturday Evening Post* on Oct. 26, 1929:

> "I'm not an atheist, and I don't think I can call myself a pantheist. We are in the position of a little child entering a huge library filled with books in many languages. The child knows someone must have written those books. It does not know how. It does not understand the languages in which they are written. The child dimly suspects a mysterious order in the arrangement of the books but doesn't know what it is. That, it seems to me, is the attitude of even the most intelligent human being toward God. We see the universe marvelously arranged and obeying certain laws, but we only dimly understand these laws. Our limited minds are not able to grasp the mysterious force that moves the constellations."

As Einstein implies, variety is the fundamental property of the universe and the brainchild of a clever and complex God. Along with energy, matter, time, and space, the world around us exists in a glorious harmony of diversity. Everything that you see (or don't see) is entirely different from anything else in the known universe. Each and every distinction, no matter how small, is a testimony to the brilliance of a Creator who never repeats Himself.

It's been suggested, in fact, by the renowned physicist Freeman Dyson that the universe was constructed according to the principle of "maximum diversity." Dyson implies that the laws of nature and its primary conditions at the beginning of creation were intended to make the universe as fascinating as possible. Apparently, the Almighty took aggressive measures to push His creativity to the extreme edge of uniqueness.

> Variety is the fundamental property of the universe and the brainchild of a clever and complex God.

Earlier scientists such as Francis Bacon, one of the founding fathers of modern science, and René Descartes, the father of modern philosophy, also shared this concept of radical diversity. Both men were well known in the sixteenth century for their views on the expanse of the universe and the diversity of creation. Descartes said:

"The universe is so rich in diversity that almost anything anyone says about it is correct."

Perhaps this quote is somewhat overstated, but great thinkers such as Einstein, Dyson, Bacon, and Descartes have brilliantly enlightened us about the uniqueness of creation. We have only to look at the vast array of stars, galaxies, and the extensive assortment of life on Earth to see that God is wholly committed to manifold expressions of creativity. The mind-boggling reality is that the Creator loves variety and has gone to great lengths to establish Himself as the architect of "maximum diversity."

The Signature of God

Clearly, the handwriting of God is seen in the vast expanse of space. There are, in fact, no duplicates in an ever-expanding universe that is roughly ninety-four million light years across, consisting of one hundred billion galaxies, each comprised of nearly one hundred billion stars. Of the trillions of objects in space, not one star, planet, or particle of stellar matter is exactly the same. This is also true of the orbital spheres of planets, the density of black holes, the nuclear forces of supernovas, and the infinite number of other anomalies in space that are truly one of a kind.

Also consistent with the theme of God's genius is the wide range of bio-diversity (the sum of all life on Earth), which covers nearly thirty million existing species on our planet. This includes roughly nine hundred thousand insects, forty-one thousand vertebrates, and two hundred-fifty thousand plants. The remainder consists of invertebrates, fungi, algae, and a host of microorganisms. Astonishingly, these species are all uniquely diverse, and like the elements of the universe, no two are exactly the same.

Then, there is the extraordinary realm of atomic diversity, which is also a testimony to God's remarkable creativity. Although invisible to the human eye, the smallest speck of matter seen under a microscope is wide enough to contain ten billion atoms. And, of the infinite number of electron orbits within these atoms, no two are exactly the same. Each varies in speed and orbital movement, traveling around the core of the nucleus at such erratic rates and patterns (making billions of trips each millionth of a second) that it's impossible to map their movement. This phenomenon, which takes place in a speck of matter that is billions of times smaller than the thickness of a human hair, plays a vital role in undergirding all existing matter in the cosmos.

Essentially, every aspect of creation screams out the vast diversity of Almighty God. Every speck of space dust, sub-atomic particle, and species of bio-diversity bears His fingerprint, and every ray of light is a reflection of His amazing creativity. In simple terms, David writes in Psalm 19:1, "The heavens are telling of the glory of God, and their expanse is declaring the work of His hands."

Now that's creative genius!

Things to Consider

As you can see, the diversity of God exists everywhere and on every level of life—visible and invisible. The sixteenth century astronomer Johannes Kepler offered a more eloquent definition when he said:

> "The diversity of the phenomena of nature is so great, and the treasures hidden in the heavens so rich, precisely in order that the human mind shall never be lacking in fresh nourishment."

Again, this means no two things in the universe function the same way, nor do they share the same features or characteristics. There are no two trees, snowflakes, raindrops, stars, planets, or galaxies that are truly identical. Although interrelated, they differ partly because of the laws of diversity found in nature and partly because it's absurd to expect a creative genius like God to duplicate true art.

Being that the Almighty is the mastermind of maximum diversity, He is incapable of repetition. Based on this truth, our recognition of diversity is critical to the way we relate to the

Creator and view the workings of His universe. If we accept the diversity of creation as being divine in origin, then we will discover the wonder of God's genius revealed in a harmonious display of intelligent design. If we ignore it, we are doomed to a mentality of sameness that is in conflict with His intention to make every aspect of creation as unique as possible.

CHAPTER

2

One of a Kind

"At bottom every man knows well enough that he is a unique being, only once on this Earth; and by no extraordinary chance will such a marvelously picturesque piece of diversity ... ever be put together the second time."

—Friedrich Nietzsche—
German philosopher and writer

Much like the diversity seen in the universe, God's creative genius is brilliantly displayed through your uniqueness as a human being.

The unshakable reality is that your life is not only unusual—but beyond ordinary. You possess rare qualities that are ever-present throughout your existence on Earth. This is true of every aspect of your being, including your conception, your complex cellular structure, and your individual personality. Also, rare beyond measure is the makeup of your intellectual, emotional, and spiritual temperament.

Why would God take such extreme measures to make you one of a kind? What were the odds of you becoming a unique

23

human being at conception? And why is it necessary to discover who you are and why you were born different?

Part of the answer lies in the reality that God is unfailingly intentional. There are simply no maybes, chances, or random occurrences in His world. Everything that *was* and *is* has been thought out long before the beginning of time, and things that *will be* already exist in the heart of the Creator. The Message Bible proclaims in Romans 8:29, "God knew what He was doing from the very beginning. He decided from the outset to shape the lives of those who love Him."

As you can see, the reality is that your special design was predetermined by God and your existence is the outcome of divine intention. You were fashioned unlike any other human and possess uncommon characteristics that make you a unique expression of the complex and marvelous mystery of life. The very moment you were conceived, you began a journey that's different from all others.

Defying the Odds

How different are you?

On a cellular level, you are comprised of approximately one hundred trillion cells, containing specific genetic information known as DNA. At conception, this genetic material, which is encoded in the structure of every cell, determines your physical features, your intellect, your emotional temperament, and the many other genetic traits that make you an exceptional human being.

> Your existence is intentional and has nothing to do with fate and everything to do with destiny.

In fact, scientists tell us that your cellular makeup is so rare that the chances of you sharing an identical

DNA fingerprint with another person are virtually impossible. Astonishingly, the odds are one in several hundred trillion.

Still, the greater miracle is the manner in which you arrive at your point of being. Medical research shows that the beginning of your existence is wrought with unthinkable perils in your mother's womb. When the sperm meets the egg, for example, it's the end of a journey of astronomical odds for survival and the beginning of a difficult voyage to grow up and become the person you were created to be. That means the odds of you becoming you are mind-boggling, considering the infinite possibilities that were present at your conception.

To put it into perspective, the scientific community tells us that women are born with about three million unfertilized eggs contained in their ovaries—each one having a different genetic profile than the others. Of this number, approximately four hundred will be actually recruited and released during her reproductive lifespan. Every month, about twenty eggs will begin a maturation process from which one dominant egg will emerge. The expectant egg, which contains specific chromosomes that carry genetic information, will sit for several days awaiting fertilization. If not fertilized, it will die and a totally different egg with a different genetic structure will take its place the following month.

The same odds apply to the role the male's sperm plays in delivering its DNA to the egg. When the sperm is released into the female, for example, nearly five hundred million of these microscopic cells begin a swimming competition toward the waiting egg. Of the five hundred million, about two hundred will survive the acidic environment and complete the risky journey to where the egg awaits fertilization. Although all two hundred will attempt to penetrate the egg, only one will succeed and block the entry to the others.

At that point, fertilization occurs. The chromosomes of the egg and the sperm intermingle and bits of genetic information from each partner unite, determining specific characteristics of the embryonic life-form. When this happens, cells begin to divide and multiply, and the development of a unique human being begins. Miraculously, that embryonic mass of little cells, barely detectable to the human eye, was you in the making.

One in Five Hundred Million

Is all this a matter of fate? Or is there embedded in the DNA of every human being a divine purpose that defies the secular notion that life is a game of luck and chance?

Of all the beliefs of the Judeo-Christian faith, one of the most staggering is the intentionality of God revealed through the life of every person. There are simply no accidents in the design and conception of our individual existence. Although every one of us began as a helpless microscopic sperm swimming in an environment that gave us one chance in five hundred million to survive, we beat these astronomical odds and became an exception to a statistical impossibility.

The good news is, those of us who survived the perilous odyssey in our mother's womb grew up to become doctors, accountants, poets, ministers, architects, lawyers, carpenters, politicians, musicians, athletes, and on goes the list. The other 499,999,999 microscopic sperm vanished forever, nameless and forgotten—never having a chance to become what they could have been. For reasons beyond our comprehension, we are here at this moment in time and they are not.

In every sense of the word, we are miracles. Regardless of the unthinkable odds that were stacked against us, our survival was divinely orchestrated by a God who had our journey in mind long before the creation of the universe. No matter how insignificant we might feel, we are here on Earth for a precise reason. Fortunately, our purpose has nothing to do with fate and everything to do with a prearranged destiny that's present throughout our entire existence.

The prophet Isaiah described it best when he surmised in Isaiah 49:1 that the Lord called him for a specific purpose in life before he was born and named him in his mother's womb. Again, this means that the Creator is intentional about every nuance of His creation and maintains a level of influence in the world that transcends mere chance. If our lives were simply a product of coincidence, then the future of the world would be dependent upon a random roll of the dice. That assumption, in my opinion, is inconsistent with the way God shapes the affairs of mankind and the role we are destined to play in the development of human history.

Embracing Your Uniqueness

In spite of our potential to live an extraordinary life, many today suffer from feelings of isolation that come from being a unique human being. At one time or another, most of us have hidden behind the delusion that our uniqueness is more of a curse than a blessing. Rather than embrace our individuality, we often stumble through this world unsure of our value and purpose in life.

How many times, for instance, have you looked up to the sky and thought, *Who am I, and why do I exist?* Have you ever been tempted to withdraw from life and simply endure a mundane existence because of the overwhelming sense of aloneness that comes from being different? Or has the raw awareness of your individuality been a blessing in disguise, providing the momentum to push you beyond the threshold of self-discovery?

For me, the journey for significance has been a long and difficult process that's spanned most of my life. Beginning at an early age, I struggled greatly with my identity as a pastor's son. Although I was ministering in our little church at five years old, I was out of sorts with my surroundings and seemed to be stifled by lifeless religiosity—unable to breathe. To make matters worse, I never fit into the social structure at school and had few friends other than my family. In every sense of the word, I was a classic loner with no sense of belonging.

Then, at the age of thirteen, I couldn't stand it any longer and took matters into my own hands. I ran away from my home in Arkansas and ended up nearly two hundred miles away in Memphis, Tennessee. Although it was a reckless thing to do, I felt I had no choice but to chase my childhood dream for significance. I seemed to be driven by a sense of unfulfilled purpose and the quest to know who I was and what I was created to do on this earth.

Needless to say, my plan to find myself didn't work out very well. Instead of connecting with my destiny, I ended up working at the State Fair running one of the games for several dollars a night. I had only one change of clothes, a single pair of socks, and very little to eat or drink. Having no place to live, I slept in the backseat of a friend's car and bathed in the sink at a nearby gas station.

Thank God, the police finally located me and returned me to my mom and dad. Nevertheless, my passion for purpose didn't subside; it only grew in intensity. A short time later, I ran away again, determined to find my place in life. By the time I was twenty years old, I had worked as an architectural draftsman, photographer, service station manager, ceramic tile setter, auto mechanic, car salesman, and house painter—while at the same time playing guitar every weekend at a local nightclub.

In spite of the many paths I traveled, however, I never lost my desire to find my ultimate destiny. No doubt, I overdid it a bit and I don't know how my parents coped with my reckless pursuit of self-discovery. But they loved me unconditionally and were convinced that I would become what they believed I was destined to become. Given enough time, they believed I would eventually embrace the God-given destiny that awaited my arrival.

Of course, a part of that destiny is the ministry I enjoy today. During the last thirty-five years, God has given me the privilege of writing several books, pastoring three churches, and traveling the world as a conference speaker. For these opportunities, I am extremely grateful and feel that I have fulfilled a significant piece of my purpose in life. Indeed, I am a blessed man with a rich heritage.

On the other hand, I understand that I have yet to reach my full potential and continually push forward to new horizons of destiny. I'm aware that this journey is not just about me and my destiny, but about the legacy that I leave behind. And regardless of the cost and inconveniences that may accompany my pursuit, I will not stop until I have lived the unique life that I was created to live. In every way, I am steadfastly committed to the discovery of my ultimate purpose on Earth—no matter where the journey leads.

Destiny by Design

In every aspect of life, our existence is a testimony to the intelligent design of the Creator. This is especially true of our distinct place in history and our contribution to the society in which we live. Because of the delicate balance needed for the unfolding of God's purpose in history, every nuance of our being is factored into the equation of life.

As I've already stated, there's no coincidence surrounding our birth or our God-breathed destiny. All that we are and will become is playing into Heaven's intention to maximize our uniqueness. Even the exact timing of our conception is critical to the makeup of our emotional, spiritual, and physical being, and determines the role we will play in society.

The scenarios throughout history are endless. For example, if Benjamin Franklin's father had not impregnated his wife on the exact month, day, and minute he did, there would be no discovery of static electricity, and the world would be sitting in total darkness. If little Benjamin had become weary and given up the swim in his mother's womb, another microscopic contender would have beaten him to the egg. That cell might have grown up to be a poet, architect, or politician, but still there would be no electricity.

If you push the scenario a little further, a more complicated set of conditions comes into play. Without the discovery of electricity, Thomas Edison could not have invented the light bulb. Computers would not exist, and the convenience of technology as we know it would be a mere fantasy. On a personal note, it would have been impossible to publish my thoughts, and you would not be reading this book.

The logical conclusion is that every person is destined to play an important role in the unfolding of God's plan for the human race. The list is long and consists of doctors, scientists, politicians, teachers, and other professionals. All of these serve the expansion of God's purpose on Earth and are foundational to the advancement of modern civilization. Without them, the human race would be severely limited.

The same is true of those destined to be machine operators, plumbers, bricklayers, carpenters, and the many others that supply the inner structure for the growth and maintenance of society. Even if there were a thousand Benjamin Franklins and Thomas Edisons, the world would still be incomplete without the many tradesmen I just mentioned. There would be no labor force—no paved roads or buildings to undergird our technical achievements. Without the distinct role of each and every person, modern civilization would not exist and we would be living in a primitive state of existence.

> You are God's divine idea, not a genetic accident.

What more can I say? You are God's idea, not a genetic accident. Whether you are a housewife, brain surgeon, janitor, or accountant, you defied one-in-five-hundred-million odds to become a life-form with destiny programmed into your DNA. When you consider those overwhelming odds, you shouldn't be here—but you are! And the way that you express your role is extremely important to satisfy God's intention for the culture in which you live.

Destiny or Choice?

Now for some difficult questions:

Is the Almighty running a monopoly on destiny? Has He predetermined the outcome of our lives so that we have little choice in what we become? Was Hitler born to be a tyrant with no choice in the matter? Did Mother Teresa champion the cause of helping suffering humanity because destiny provided no other option? And what about you? Is your own role in life a matter of destiny or choice?

Certainly, God preordains all that is good in a person's life and opposes that which is morally wrong. The fact that some people turn out to be evil doesn't mean they have no choice in the matter, nor does it mean they are without a positive life-purpose, preordained by God. The sad truth is that evil men and women choose their path—the path does not choose them. Because they are unwilling to walk in their God-ordained destiny, dark forces at work in the world provide them with an alternate course in life. By ignoring their divine calling, they often go where they were never meant to go.

For this very reason, it's imperative that we pursue our God-given destiny and not leave it to fate. We must not be fooled into thinking that if we do nothing, everything will work out perfectly. Just because we are each called to live a meaningful life doesn't mean we are without a choice in the outcome of our journey. As previously mentioned, the fulfillment of our destiny is dependent upon our decision to become the moral and wholesome person the Creator has designed us to be.

By now, the conclusion should be apparent. Destiny is not a matter of chance, but a delicate blend of divine intention and human choice. The message here is that we intentionally choose what God has preordained us to become and then deliberately walk out that decision. In this regard, predestination and free will are like a game of cards. The hand that is dealt to us is predestination. The way we choose to play that hand is free will. Together, these two dynamics complete the full circle of life that we are meant to live—from the cradle to the grave.

Things to Consider

Whether on a conscious or subconscious level, the struggle to accept our own individuality is present in every person. I know it's difficult, but don't become discouraged. Instead, remind yourself that every breath you take is a once-in-a-lifetime gift from God that makes you an extraordinary human being. Like a lone beacon shining in the darkness of night, your existence is a rare reflection of the Creator's unique artistry.

Then again, the central issue is not how different you are, but how willing you are to express your own individuality in a world suffocating from an ideology of sameness. Will you hide from the opportunity to celebrate the rare and extraordinary uniqueness of your existence? Or will you live a life that is beyond ordinary?

The award-winning fashion designer and photographer Sir Cecil Beaton clearly addressed this issue when he said:

> "Be daring, be different, be impractical, be anything that will assert integrity of purpose and imaginative vision against the play-it-safers, the creatures of the commonplace, the slaves of the ordinary."

To put it another way, let the world know who you are, not what they want you to be. Dare to be open and real! And most importantly, dare to be yourself. Considering that you only have one life to live, it might as well be your own.

Honestly, your failure to become what you are intended to be is costly beyond imagination. According to Romans 8, the whole creation awaits the discovery of your unique role as a human being and is held captive by your decision to express (or not express) your individuality. Also, being who you are made to be is vital to the way God reveals His diverse and complex personality to an on-looking world.

3

Reflections of Divinity

"In every concrete individual, there is a uniqueness that defies formulation. We can feel the touch of it and recognize its face... but we can give no ultimate account of it... we have in the end simply to admire the Creator."

—William James—
American philosopher and writer

Throughout the formative years of my life, I spent a lot of time thinking about the different aspects of God's creative genius. As an adult, however, my focus began to turn from fascination to desperation. My most passionate prayer was that I could somehow experience the Creator's uniqueness in a manner that is beyond mere theology. I'm not really sure if I knew what I was asking, but I was simply desperate to see a diverse yet tangible reflection of the Lord's face in creation.

While contemplating these things one Saturday evening, something extraordinary began to unfold in my heart. I had a strong gut feeling that my prayer was going to be answered. Intuitively, I felt it would happen the following day—right before I delivered my Sunday morning message. Right away, I began to prepare my heart for a revelation about God's reflection through humanity that would radically transform my life.

Needless to say, I was thrilled! In fact, I was so excited that I ran three stop signs driving to church the next morning. Finally, after being pulled over by a police officer, I apologized for breaking the law and admitted that I was a pastor in a hurry to get to church. To my surprise, the officer simply admonished me and let me go without writing a ticket. Embarrassed by his warning, I drove away feeling somewhat humbled.

By the time I arrived at church, however, I had forgotten the entire incident. I could hardly wait to get on the platform and sit down in my chair behind the pulpit. By no means was I going to miss what I felt would be one of the greatest revelations of my life. *And, what a great place for it to happen,* I thought, *right here on Sunday morning in the house of God.*

Seeing God's Face

Now breathless with anticipation, I closed my eyes tightly during the first part of the service, waiting for the promised encounter. Although I wasn't sure if I would see a vision or fall under some kind of heavenly trance, I was sure of two things: I was ready for the experience and fully aware of the impact it would have on my life.

> To see God's face, you must simply look into the faces of those made in His image.

As my moment of discovery drew near, I heard an inner voice say, "Do you want to see the manifestation of My glory? Are you ready to see My face? If you are, then open your eyes and look around the room."

Eagerly, I opened both eyes, only to hear the voice say, "What do you see?" In my mind, I replied, *"Lord, I see nothing but a lot of people."*

When there was no reply, I closed my eyes again, thinking I had somehow missed my cue. Once again I heard the voice say, "Open your eyes and tell Me what you see." This time I replied in more detail, *"I see people, all kinds of people. I see white faces, black faces, brown faces, young faces, and old faces."*

Then almost audibly, I heard the words, "You have just seen My face. You have seen the greatest manifestation of My glory that you will ever see while on Earth." At that moment, I knew that to see God's face, I simply had to look at the faces of those made in His image. Instantly, I remembered the time in the Bible when Philip asked to see God and Jesus replied in John 14:9, "He who has seen Me has seen the Father."

At first, I must admit that I was caught off guard. Then as the revelation slowly settled into my spirit, I began to fall apart—unable to contain my love for the people in front of me. I left church that day with a profound appreciation for all of humanity and vowed to never again make the mistake of dissociating God's glory from His creation.

I also realized that I couldn't claim to love God if I was not willing to esteem those made in His image. I realized how offensive it would be to say to an artist, "I like you, but I don't like the images you have created." Deep inside, I knew this kind of insensitivity would be the ultimate insult—especially to the Creator of the universe.

Reflections

More than thirty years have passed since that glorious day, and I feel that I've only begun to understand the uniqueness of God in mankind. The more I study the Bible, the more I'm convinced that the Creator is at work enlarging our capacity to reflect His multifaceted personality. Beginning with Adam and Eve, His intention has always been to fully disclose Himself by pouring His diverse being into "jars of clay."

In symbolic terms, such an attempt by the Lord to reveal Himself to humanity is seen throughout much of the Old Testament. As recorded in Exodus 25-28, the "Ancient of Days" revealed to Moses a precise blueprint for the construction of a desert tabernacle, adorned with an extensive selection of colors and materials that were designed to reflect different facets of God's personality. It is widely taught that the color red spoke of His passionate love; blue represented His revelatory Spirit, and purple served as a reminder of His royal nature.

Yet, in my view, the most striking aspect of God's person was represented by the colorful breastplate worn by the High Priest. As described in Exodus 28:15-30, this ornate piece of clothing was made of pure gold and lavishly adorned with twelve precious stones, each representing one of the twelve tribes of Israel. Many believe, in fact, that the distinct colors and characteristics of the stones and the tribal names engraved on them were symbolic reflections of the Almighty's multi-dimensional personality seen in each tribe.

It could be assumed, for example, that the brilliance of the diamond represented God's radiant nature in the tribe of Gad, while the red sardius demonstrated the bloodline of Jesus in Judah. It's also reasonable to surmise that the blue sapphire conveyed the revelatory spirit of Simeon, and the purple amethyst symbolized the royal character of Benjamin. As for the remaining eight stones, they also revealed other unique aspects of God's divine nature.

What is truly amazing to me, however, is the imagery of the High Priest standing before God wearing the breastplate as a symbolic representation of His people. As described in Exodus 28, he would enter the inner chamber of the tabernacle, fully adorned with the breastplate and elaborate garments of red, blue, and purple. Alone in the solitary darkness, the colorfully clad priest stood before the presence of the Lord as a reminder of God's collective glory that was resident in the ancient Hebrew tribes.

In a larger context, the High Priest was also a distinct prototype of Christ's priesthood in the New Testament. By that I mean the first was literal and the latter spiritual. In simpler terms, just as the colorful breastplate of the Old Testament priest represented the different aspects of the Creator's nature reflected through the Israelites, the priestly heart of Jesus reflects the diverse individuality of New Testament believers.

The Spectrum

Although I highly value Old Testament symbolism, I'm also aware that mystical imagery is probably not the best way to present God's diversity to a postmodern world. In hopes of reaching a broader audience, therefore, I recently decided to look at God's uniqueness from a different perspective and turned my attention to the science of light and color. I began to explore the basic properties of natural light as it relates to the different expressions of color in the physical world.

I discovered, for example, that light is made up of energy particles called photons that travel in the form of waves. When we use the term "light," therefore, we are referring to a type of electromagnetic wave that is visible to the human eye. Other wave frequencies such as microwave, radio, infrared, x-rays, ultraviolet, and gamma rays that are invisible to the human eye, are also part of the entire spectrum. Together these visible and invisible spectrums make up the full property of light as we know it today.

I also revisited several facts about the spectrum of light that many of us learned in school. I remembered that our present-day understanding of light and color began with Isaac Newton and a series of experiments he published in 1672. Regarding the spectrum of visible light, Newton was the first to suggest that light from the Sun is made of various colors. He set out to prove that objects appear to be a certain color because of how they reflect light, rather than color being an inherent property of an object. His theory was that each individual wavelength within the spectrum of visible light is representative of a particular color. He basically believed that the signature of color is the wavelength of light.

To prove the theory, Newton used an experimental concept to analyze the natural properties of light. In his research, he discovered that sunlight refracted through a prism could be split into a spectrum of seven visible colors: red, orange, yellow, green, blue, indigo, and violet. Newton referred to the spreading of these rays as *dispersion* and called the different colors of rays the *spectrum*. The spectrum, he wrote, is a "continuum of colors tinged with a series of color together with all their indeterminate degrees in a continuing succession, perpetually varying."

Regarding his celebrated "phenomenon of color," Newton also found that light rays passed back through the prism turned once again into white light. His conclusion was that white is not a color wavelength in itself, but is simply the presence of all colors. His groundbreaking research clearly demonstrated that light alone is responsible for color and is alive with a vast range of diversity.

The Colors of God

At last, the revelation I received as a young man began to come together in my mind. "God is light!" In James 1:17, He is called the Father of lights, and in John 1:9, He is known as the true light that enlightens every person who comes into the world. John also writes in Revelation 22:5 that God is the light that illuminates those who pass on to the next life.

The obvious conclusion is that God and light are one. They are inseparable entities—each one irreversibly and eternally linked to the other. Just as the color spectrum is made up of individual reflections of light waves in the physical world, the light of God also radiates unique expressions of spiritual color that are dispersed throughout all of humanity. When we're exposed to this divine light of God, the colors of the unseen world are reflected through us in a broad spectrum of diversity—much like the light that is refracted through a prism.

> Like the colors of the rainbow, the splendor of God is reflected through humanity in a broad spectrum of beauty.

In simple terms, each and every person radiates a unique spectrum of spiritual color that was in God's heart long before the beginning of time. There are no exceptions or exclusions. As mentioned in chapter two, the Bible makes it clear that we were chosen by God before the foundation of the world and are predestined to express a piece of His unique nature. Before we were conceived in our mother's womb, we were called to be glorious reflections of God's Son.

Perhaps this was the reason that my soul was deeply moved as a child by the song "This Little Light of Mine." Now that I think about it, every time I sang the chorus, "This little light of mine, I'm gonna let it shine," God was speaking to me about His unique nature in my life. He seemed to be telling me about the intrinsic value of my individuality and the vast assortment of humanity needed to manifest His diversity in the earth.

Apparently, God wants the truth of this song to live big in my heart today. Recently, in fact, I've been hearing the melody in my head and feel compelled to unleash my light whenever and wherever I can. And no matter how small my "little light" may be when compared to the brightness of other personalities, I'm learning that it represents a distinct color of God that I alone possess. Regardless of my imperfections, I am a once-in-a-lifetime expression of His extraordinary creativity. Like one of the gemstones that adorned the breastplate of the high priest, my whole being is a partial, yet colorful reflection of God's divine nature.

Things to Consider

Perhaps the greatest revelation we will see in this life is God's reflection in the faces of people. To ignore these divine reflections is to hide from the One who breathed His creativity into humanity. As I've already said, we have been handcrafted in the likeness of God and are privileged to bear His divine profile. Isaiah 43:7 declares that we are His people, called by His name and created as a display of His glory.

The New Testament also deals with this subject and unveils a diversity of gifts given to us by the Holy Spirit. Paul clearly points out in 1 Corinthians 12 that we all function differently and possess different aspects of God's nature—even though we are one body of believers. In the Easy-to-Read Version of the Bible, Paul instructs us in verse six that:

> "There are different ways God works in our lives, but it is the same God who does the work through all of us."

The unshakable truth is that God's glorious person has been distributed in a diverse manner among those willing to host His presence. To help frame this concept in everyday terms, we must embrace the broad range of diversity that the Creator has invested in each and every person. At first glance, these unique reflections may seem contradictory to each other, but at their core is the potential for unity beyond anything we have ever known. As we will explore in Part Two, individuality that is God-centered and rooted in self-acceptance is perhaps our greatest hope for the future.

PART
TWO

Discovering the Uniqueness of God in Your Existence

CHAPTER

4

The Divine Embrace

"The first step in becoming who you are
created to be is to love and accept
yourself as God loves and
accepts you."

—Larry Randolph—

Throughout Part One, I presented a broad-stroke picture of God's intelligent design in creation. I also made the case for the Creator's uniqueness in humanity and the role that each of us plays in reflecting a piece of His persona. My purpose was to make you aware of our extraordinary uniqueness and the intentionality of our design.

In Part Two, my primary goal is to reveal the significance of our worth as human beings and to uncover the reality of our authentic existence. In order to accomplish this task, however, I must first deal with a complex issue that's hard for most people to comprehend. The crux of this issue is that God wants us to feel loved. The irony, however, is that we seem to be incapable of loving ourselves as He loves us.

Why is it so difficult to embrace the affection of a Creator who made us after His likeness?

The problem, in my opinion, is not in our perception that God is love, but lies in our inability to receive His love for our own lives. Unfortunately, we build churches and religious organizations based on the concept of a loving Creator, but we seldom experience His unconditional love on a personal level. Somehow we have missed the critical link between loving God and the command in Matthew 22:37-39 to love your neighbor as yourself.

Self-affection or Self-rejection?

As a child, I was deeply conflicted about the issue of self-acceptance. I had no problem with the "love others" command, but the commandment to love myself truly baffled my soul. Even as a young pastor, the nearly impossible command seemed to cut across the grain of my performance-based upbringing. I'm sad to say that I was nearly forty years old before I began to appreciate my worth as a child of God.

Unfortunately, this problem is not limited to me alone but is rampant throughout much of my family. Several years ago, my bi-racial grandson was depressed about his unique features and skin color. When my daughter told me about his negative self-image, I was painfully aware of the unresolved issues in our family that keep us from loving ourselves. We understand intellectually that God places greater value on the heart than on the outward appearance. Yet most of my family members, including myself, find it easier to love what we see in others rather than embrace our own worth as human beings.

As mentioned earlier, there are many believers who struggle with this issue today. Extremely problematic is the flawed theology about our value as members of God's family. Instead of building self-esteem that is anchored in the unconditional love and acceptance that's available in Christ, we've fostered a religious mindset that seems to equate self-abasement with humility. In many religious circles we are mistakenly taught that the more we disconnect from our earthly nature and detest our humanity, the more God will approve of us. Needless to say, this deceptive mindset undermines our value as treasured sons and daughters of God.

In short, this deception not only devalues God's intentions for humanity, but is harmful to the advancement of His kingdom on Earth. Quite frankly, the danger that we face is not satanism or humanism—it is our willingness to surrender the concept of self-love to the New Age movement and self-help groups that target mainstream society. In many ways, the Church has handed over the privilege of presenting God's love to a hurting world and has settled for a gospel that no longer embraces self-acceptance as a part of its belief system.

Negative Body Image

The inability to love and accept ourselves is not only a spiritual issue, but a cultural problem that exists throughout much of the modern world. Everywhere you turn, there's an indication that average-looking people don't measure up to the high premium placed on a perfect body and profile.

Every day, we are bombarded with commercials, billboards, and magazines of perfectly proportioned people who remind us of our not-so-perfect appearance. And because of the unrealistic value placed on our looks, many have developed a negative body image that is mentally and socially unhealthy.

Regrettably, this problem has reached epidemic proportions in the world today—especially in popular American culture. There is, in fact, a sweeping misconception in this nation that we cannot feel good about ourselves until we look perfect on the outside. For the most part, our self-worth is measured by the shape of our body and the way we dress and wear our hair, not by what we are inside. The illusion is that those with a trendy look or perfect body are more likely to have a successful existence—while average-looking people who are not "fashion friendly" are exposed to a toxic grade of self-loathing.

Tragically, this lethal combination of low self-esteem and a negative body image is largely responsible for much of the mental and emotional instability that is prevalent in today's culture. Feeling hopeless and dejected, people who internalize their inability to produce a perfect appearance frequently suffer from depression, anxiety, schizophrenia, and a host of other emotional and psychological disorders. Instead of embracing their striking uniqueness, many are lured into deep mental distress and end up hating themselves.

Who is to blame for the deceptive standard that's found in today's society?

Certainly, we are all responsible for nurturing our own self-worth. Then again, we are strongly influenced by those who have raised the "beauty bar" to an unrealistic level. Sadly, the audience for this impossible standard is a generation of self-effacing women who compare themselves with movie stars and magazine models who are paid to produce the perfect profile.

In a survey by Dove soap, for example, the backlash is revealed in the negative way that everyday women view the size and shape of their nose, mouth, eyes, feet, breasts, and other parts of the body. In the survey, ladies around the globe were asked what they thought of their looks. Surprisingly, only two percent of the women described themselves as beautiful and nine percent considered themselves attractive. Another forty-three percent of the women used the term "natural," and twenty-four percent said they had average looks.

The survey is staggering and partly explains the busy schedules of the nearly five thousand cosmetic surgeons in our nation. Millions of Americans will spend billions of dollars this year on a variety of surgical procedures that are designed to change their appearance and bring to life their fantasy image. As recently reported by the American Society for Aesthetic Plastic Surgery, the top five surgical procedures for women are liposuction, breast augmentation, eyelid surgery, tummy tuck, and facelift. Also, an increasing number of men are undergoing various cosmetic procedures including nose reconstruction, breast reduction, and hair restoration.

Esteem Makeover!

Which, if any, of these procedures are acceptable, and which are considered to be vanity?

I highly respect the art of cosmetic surgery and I'm truly grateful for the procedures that are available to people with severe deformities and birth defects. I'm also appreciative of the reconstructive surgery that's performed on those disfigured by accidents and other trauma. Furthermore, I believe cosmetic surgery that targets the negative effects of aging in older people can be helpful—as long as it doesn't become an idol.

> Most of us need an "esteem makeover" rather than an "extreme makeover" of our appearance.

Even so, most of the people I know would benefit more from an "esteem makeover" of the inner-self than an "extreme makeover" of the outer-self. As much as I respect the desire of my generation to maintain a youthful appearance, we must guard ourselves against an unhealthy obsession with our looks. After all, extreme alterations of our bodies for the sake of vanity can be an insult to the Creator who made us uniquely different from all others.

This truth was made real to me when I first started dating my wife, Laura. I had always disliked my somewhat pointy nose and was self-conscious around her most of the time. I was remorseful that I didn't have a more perfect face for her to view. Several weeks into the relationship, however, Laura floored me with a confession. She said, "I love the profile of your face, especially your nose. I've always been attracted to men with strong noses like yours. It really speaks of strength and character."

That did it for me! From that moment on, I was completely disarmed, like putty in her hands. In spite of what I thought about myself, I knew she loved me just the way God made me—including my interesting nose. With God's help, I began to see that I was more in need of a "faith lift" than a "face lift." Of course, I am a long way from being handsome by society's standards. But if my wife recognizes something uniquely attractive about me, then I must have faith in the artistry of the Creator who sees His creation as wonderfully and marvelously made in His image.

The same thing applies to Laura. Although she is incredibly beautiful, there are things about her appearance that she complains about now and then. Recently, when she was feeling insecure about growing older, I reminded her that she is aging beautifully and doesn't need to alter anything. Honestly, I can't think of one thing I would change about her appearance. I love her just the way she is, and my heart often skips a beat when she walks into a room. She is truly an extraordinary gift sent straight from Heaven—a one-of-a-kind beauty whom the Creator has entrusted to me.

"Ain't I Something?"

Some of the greatest lessons that I've learned about self-acceptance have come through several of my closest friends. One of the most memorable lessons came from an extraordinary prophet named Bob Jones.

Bob is eighty years old and has a pleasant, down-to-earth Southern disposition that qualifies him to be every child's favorite grandfather. He has a head full of glistening white hair, an unforgettable voice, a warm smile, and a well-rounded profile that makes him, as my wife puts it, "just adorable." When you meet this delightful man for the first time, his cheerful personality will immediately capture your heart.

Bob is not theologically trained or eloquent in speech. Nor does he always take the time to explain in detail his many visions and encounters with God. Even so, Bob's rich history with the supernatural realm makes him one of the foremost prophetic fathers in the earth today. Like many others, I have learned priceless lessons from his life experiences and have *caught* more of God's Spirit from this man than I will ever understand intellectually.

Just recently, while speaking at a conference with Bob and his wife, Bonnie, I was taught an invaluable lesson that reflects the theme of this chapter. It all started the first night of the meeting. To get from our hotel to the conference room, we had to walk through a long hallway that was covered with mirrors from the floor to the ceiling. It was just horrible! Laura and I were extremely disturbed by our reflections in a wall of mirrors that revealed every single nuance of our profiles. Every time we passed through the "Hall of Horrors" (as we called it), we would begin to complain and look in another direction until we reached the meeting room.

By the last evening, Bob had enough of our grumbling and took the opportunity to teach us a lesson. Halfway down the corridor, he insisted that we stop and view ourselves in the mirror. To our amusement, he began to pose like a model, turning sideways to capture a full view of his profile. Then with a twinkle in his eye, he patted his somewhat ample belly with both hands and said, "Look at me! Ain't I something? I am altogether lovely! And, my Daddy made me perfect, just the way He likes me. O-h-h-h, I am so beautiful to my Papa— and so are both of you!"

I thought, *What in the world does he mean? Does he really believe he is attractive and that God loves him that much? Who told him he could be so happy with himself?*

Then it hit me like a ton of bricks. I realized the critical difference between me and this extraordinary man. Although I loved people, I lacked a clear revelation of God's unconditional embrace in my own life and was constantly battling low self-esteem. Bob, on the other hand, is comfortable in his own skin and truly believes that God delights in him being what he's created to be.

> If I am created in the image of God, then a part of God looks like me.

Somehow, he's captured the reality that he is a unique reflection of God's creative artistry—even though many in the world might consider him to be ordinary. In spite of his human imperfections, Bob is absolutely convinced that "Papa God" (as Bob often calls Him) loves him exactly the way he is and sees him as beautiful.

As you might suspect, I left the meeting with a strong sense of conviction. My soul was arrested by the revelation that Bob possessed and I knew that in order to survive the rest of my life, I had to come to terms with my worth as a unique individual. Somehow, I had to shake off the self-loathing that had plagued me since childhood and learn the lesson of God's divine embrace. And regardless of cost or inconvenience, I was determined to hang out with this amazing man until I caught the revelation he carries.

The Apple of God's Eye

Over the years, Bob has demonstrated to me the nearly in-comprehensible truth of self-acceptance. I know that Bob is not vain, nor does he base his self-worth on his appearance. Even so, he does have a keen awareness of his value as a human being and has learned to resist the lie that he's anything less than "the apple of God's eye."

By Bob's example, I'm learning the importance of this truth and know that the ultimate deception is to say I love God and yet despise myself. I'm beginning to understand that if I am created in God's image, then a part of God looks like me. This means to truly love God, I must love myself—there's just no way around it. Regardless of my flaws and limitations, I am compelled to embrace all that I am, both human and divine.

Am I suggesting that we tolerate the sins of our fallen nature that are offensive to God? Should we ignore the character flaws and weaknesses that prevent us from growing into maturity and living a life of integrity?

Of course, we all need to change the things in our hearts that hinder our spiritual growth. But there is only so much we can do about the basic way our bodies are made and the way we look. Paul clearly addressed this issue in Romans 9:20 and declared that the thing molded should not say to the molder, "Why did you make me this way?" He further stated in verse twenty-one that the Master Potter has a right to make from the same lump of clay, vessels that are different in appearance.

In many ways, this reality was demonstrated through the humanity of Jesus of Nazareth. To everyone's surprise, Isaiah 53:2 predicted that the coming Messiah would not be especially good-looking or have a striking physique that would attract people to Him. Although He was the incarnation of the Most High God, He was predestined to live in an average-looking body. Apparently, He accepted Himself as God's treasured Son and embraced His ordinary appearance as an expression of His Father's unique artistry.

As sons and daughters of God, we must also accept who and what we are in appearance. Like our Lord, we should be comfortable with the uniqueness of our individuality. We must resist the lie that our physical features are somehow flawed and that we need to change the way we are made. If we embrace this reality, we will be able to see divinity in the face of each and every person—even when we look in the mirror.

Things to Consider

It's alarming how many people go through life without learning the lessons illustrated in this chapter. Most are blind to the reality that self-hatred is a black hole that sucks all the light of self-esteem into a dark abyss of despair, making it impossible for one ray of hope to escape. They have somehow failed to recognize that self-loathing is a form of emotional abuse—which is by nature an insult to the Creator who made them after His image and likeness.

As we've discussed, the opposite is true of self-acceptance. Saint Augustine put it beautifully when he said, "He who is filled with love is filled with God Himself." I agree with this simple message and believe that our capacity to receive and release God's love is limited only by our capacity to love ourselves. If we cannot love ourselves, it's extremely difficult to love God or His creation. The bottom line, according to Mother Teresa, is that "God has created us to love and to be loved."

Again, this simple reality only highlights our need to break the vicious cycle of self-loathing that keeps us from seeing the divine in humanity. Clearly, it's the act of loving and accepting ourselves that enables us to embrace the Creator and touch our destiny through the salvation of His Son.

5

Authentic Existence

*"It is the chiefest point of happiness that
a man is willing to be what he is."*

—Desiderius Erasmus—
Dutch humanist and theologian

In the same way that you embrace your unique appearance, you must also accept your distinct individuality. Your ultimate purpose in life is achieved by being true to who you are, not by emulating the qualities you admire in others. This means your authentic existence—which is a blend of character, personality, gifting, and other unique aspects of your being—is a priceless gift that you alone possess.

Even so, it's one thing to talk about being authentic and another thing to understand the concept of authenticity on both a practical and philosophical level. On a practical level, most encyclopedias and dictionaries tell us that authenticity refers to truthfulness of origin within a concept or thing and is simply the absence of all falsification and forgery. In regard to creative skills such as the arts and music, authenticity demands certain commitments to originality and points to a clarity of distinction and uniqueness that is indisputable.

As for the philosophical concept, the notion of authenticity as related to human existence is a bit more complicated. It's difficult to determine the origin of the contemporary idea of authenticity other than its use as a clinical term in existentialist philosophy. This philosophy, which is separate from orthodox religion, approaches the meaning of life from a humanistic viewpoint that is committed to the absolute sovereignty of a person's own self-interest.

In fact, a number of substitutes to traditional religion have emerged in the last century, such as the existentialist view of self that I just mentioned. This view is widely proclaimed by existentialists who emphasize significance through subjectivity as their designer brand of salvation. The goal of the existentialist is to find their individual identity and freedom in a total commitment to their own agenda.

In fact, many existentialists see the conscious self as being unique and separate from everyone and everything in the world. This philosophy maintains the belief that the authentic man will never be satisfied playing a role or being a cog in the machinery of industrial society—but is only free when he reaches total independence. Authenticity, in this regard, is determined by the degree to which a person is true to one's own existence without consideration of God or others.

The Authenticity Zone

Now for my simple view of authentic existence:

First and foremost, I strongly disagree with the philosophy that authenticity is achieved by merely finding and embracing one's self. As already stated, this version of salvation is self-centered and leaves no room for loving God or people. By nature, it's a dangerous form of narcissism that's foreign to the personality of an affectionate Creator, underscoring a lifestyle that's meaningless and totally self-serving.

On the contrary, true authenticity is attained when we find God within ourselves and embrace the reality that the two (God and man) can become one. In this framework of truth, we discover that it's our association with Christ that gives us authentic life, not merely the awareness of self. In every way, this God-connection sets us apart from the flawed philosophy of modern existentialism and helps us discover who we were created to be through oneness with the Creator.

In simple terms, a truly authentic existence is having a God-focus instead of a self-focus. You become who you are only when you discover who you are in the company of God. Your potential, gifting, and ultimate destiny are all tied to your fellowship with the Creator. Ultimately, who and what you are emerges as you interact relationally with a God who is eager to shape the reality of your present and future. Consequently, the authentic self you find in the process is expressed through the unique contributions you make in life and the role you play in the development of society.

In this regard, modern man has two choices: You can play in the sandbox of existentialist philosophy and live for yourself. Or you can embrace your authentic existence and find *true* meaning in life.

If you choose the first option, you will undoubtedly live without purpose—stumbling through the world as a testimony to the hopelessness of self without God. Your existence, though precious, will be a mere shadow of the God-centered life that you were destined to live.

If you choose the latter, your life will matter. You will rise above the boredom of mediocrity and find the true meaning of your existence. From this place of authentic living, a sense of destiny will emerge. There will be a heightened perception that you are original by design. Every nuance of your being will scream out your uniqueness, revealing that your life is a special gift to the world.

This is authentic existence at its very best!

Becoming You

Of equal importance is the responsibility to express your individuality. It's simply not enough to realize the value of your authenticity or your God-given uniqueness. You must live out who you are in front of others.

> It's impossible for anyone but you to contribute to the world what you alone can give.

Why? Because if you fail to express the unique part of God that has been deposited in your life, the world will never see that particular aspect of His character. When you die, the once-in-a-lifetime mix of God's divine nature and your distinct personality will die with you. All that remains will be a lost opportunity of what the Creator might have looked like in a life yielded to His artistic creativity.

Furthermore, that particular reflection of God through your unique existence can never be recaptured by anyone else at any point in time or history. Others will try, and they may be able to do what you do somewhat like you do it. But they will never do what you do better than you do it, or exactly the way you do it. They are limited by the *absence* of your unique gifting, your distinct personality, and the original breath of life that makes you truly extraordinary. These limitations make it impossible for anyone else to contribute to this world what you alone have to give.

As a child, I saw this reality played out in the life of a unique man who understood what it meant to be himself. His name was James Randolph. He was my mentor, my pastor, and most importantly, he was my father. By example, he taught me the value of being myself and demonstrated to me the futility of conforming to a world stuck in a mindset of sameness. He was determined to find out what God made him to be and frequently encouraged me to do the same.

Dad was different! In fact, many in our church thought he was different to the point of stubbornness. The problem was that my father lived in an era of loud preaching and pulpit theatrics but refused to imitate the preaching style of his day. Long before it was kosher, Dad spoke softly in the pulpit with his hands stuck in his pants pockets. He never yelled or made sudden moves and often talked affectionately about the love of God with tears streaming down his face. As you would expect, his gentle demeanor was an extreme contradiction to the loud, judgmental preaching that seemed to be characteristic of our Pentecostal denomination.

My father was also different in many other aspects of life. Although he had very little education, his emotional and spiritual IQ was literally off the charts. As a human being and a minister, he was amazingly authentic, true to his own heart, and dared to be himself. Like a fish swimming upstream, Dad lived by his own convictions. He preferred to suffer the isolation of rejection for being real rather than faking it so he could be accepted by his peers.

Peculiar but Original

Another attribute of my father's personality was his offbeat sense of humor. Every now and then, he would do things that were totally "out of the box."

One of my fondest memories happened on Easter Sunday at a luncheon in our front yard. A large number of our relatives were present, including my aunts, uncles, cousins, and two of my grandparents. When the atmosphere grew tense from a lack of conversation, Dad quickly disappeared into the house. To our surprise, he emerged a few minutes later dressed up like a Native American chief. He was wearing my mother's necklace with a blanket wrapped around his shoulders. On his head was a cheap headband he had purchased at a dime store and a large feather stuck in the side of his hair. In an exaggerated tone of voice, he began to talk to us in a made-up dialect.

As expected, our family didn't know how to respond, other than to stare at the ground and blink our eyes. My mother, who was shy by nature, was totally embarrassed and could only mumble, "Oh, James, you're so silly." However, I thought it was extremely funny and began to chuckle under my breath. To this day, I still smile every single time I think about the boring Easter dinner that was spiced up by Dad's weird sense of humor.

Why did Dad do things like that? I'm not really sure, except that he lived in a church culture that was overly serious to the point of boredom. Perhaps it was his way of getting out of the religious box and letting off some creative steam. Or perhaps it was just his way of breaking the icy chill among our uptight family members.

Whatever the reason, I have always admired Dad's quirky personality and have been accused of being a "chip off the old block." For that, I am proud to be my father's son. By his example, I've learned to value my own unique sense of humor. I'm beginning to see that it's not about the way I decide to present God, but about the way God wants to present Himself through me—even if that presentation reflects the lighter side of my personality.

Perhaps my father overdid it from time to time, but he gave me the courage to be myself—no matter how different that may appear. And though he passed away with few people knowing he ever existed, he was truly one of a kind. In fact, the memory of his unique life is ever-present in my thoughts, reminding me that I can live as an original in a world of copycats.

The Real Thing

Several years ago, while pondering Dad's life, I remembered a phrase he and my grandfather often used. When referring to someone or something they believed was authentic, they would say, "That's the real McCoy." They seemed to have an unusual ability to recognize things that were genuine and could spot a fake a mile away.

> To experience an authentic life, you must live as an original in a world full of copycats.

Now that I think about it, I doubt if either Dad or Granddad understood the origin of this obscure phrase. With a little research, however, I quickly discovered that "the real McCoy" is an old expression used throughout much of the English-speaking world meaning "the real thing." It denotes a person, thing, or state of being that is authentically original. When people say, "That's the real McCoy," they are saying it's the "genuine article."

Even though the origin of this idiom is somewhat obscure, many people claim that the saying "the real McCoy" came from the name of the American boxer, Kid McCoy, who held the welterweight championship title in the late 1800s. He was widely known as a fast and powerful fighter who would cut down his opponents with devastating blows.

It's alleged, for example, that the famous McCoy had so many imitators who took his name in boxing that he eventually billed himself as "The Real McCoy." One story tells about a tough guy who was pestering McCoy in a bar. When someone told him that the man he was harassing was Kid McCoy, the famous boxer, he laughed and challenged the champion to a fight. After being knocked out by a devastating punch, the bully finally regained consciousness and mumbled, "Oh, my God. That was the real McCoy."

What value does this story hold for a modern world overrun with countless imitations and impersonations? For the most part, people who are raised in a culture of counterfeits have a low tolerance for any degree of pretense. This is especially true of today's younger generation and explains the reason for much of their discontentment. They are typically bored with anything that appears fake and seem to harbor a deep desire for things that are authentic.

As a teenager, I, too, was attracted to authenticity. In fact, the first time I heard the Coca Cola jingle, "It's the real thing," I was compelled to switch my soda preference overnight. The attraction had little to do with the taste of the beverage and everything to do with the idea that I could experience something better than an imitation. Although it was little more than a marketing ploy, I was easily hooked and more than willing to alter my lifestyle for something real.

The same is true of my life today. Although I have mellowed out a bit, my passion for originality is still the driving force behind everything I do. You can call it a desire to be "the real McCoy" or a thirst for "the real thing." But like Dad, I would rather be a nameless original than a famous copy. In fact, I'll go to almost any length to avoid impersonations of life that are disingenuous. Thankfully, I've learned to value the difference between originality and cheap imitations.

Parroting Others

Several years ago, I had a conversation with a friend that stirred my thinking about the issue of authenticity. He told me an amusing story about a preacher who owned a pet parrot.

According to my friend, the minister held Friday night prayer meetings in the living room where the parrot was caged. Without giving it a thought, he often left the cage uncovered, exposing the bird to the sights and sounds of the meeting.

One Saturday morning, the minister awoke to a strange sound coming from the parrot's cage. When he looked into the living room, the parrot was swaying from side to side on his perch, singing a hymn ever so softly. At that point, the bird abruptly stopped his singing and began to strut back and forth on the perch shouting and praying loudly. After a few minutes of thunderous prayer, he went back to singing reverently, swaying back and forth to the chorus, "Hallelujah, hallelujah."

I was both amused and troubled by the parrot story. Like the parrot's owner, I have also witnessed impersonations of spirituality that were entertaining but insincere. In fact, many of the sermons I've heard from the pulpit are little more than echoes of other people's experiences. No doubt, the majority of these impersonations come from a genuine attempt to convey truth. But for the most part, they are strikingly unoriginal and lack the passion that comes from true creativity.

Regarding this issue, the following questions have recently been troubling my heart. Are we to ignore the valuable life lessons of others? Or can we take ownership of another person's experience and use their specific language and mannerisms to communicate truth?

To be honest, my thoughts about the issue have been mixed in the past. Certainly there is nothing wrong with borrowed truth—especially truth that's become real to your own heart. In most cases, the life-changing truths of men and women that are passed from generation to generation carry the very essence of their spirit and soul. For example, the first century disciples of Christ emulated the attribute and sayings of their Master, and as a result, His teachings were preserved throughout history by a transfer of spirit and truth.

All the same, there are other factors that must be taken into consideration. While it's a blessing to gather and dispense the revelation of others, we must be aware of its limitations. There is a striking difference between expressing truth that is real to your heart and mechanically repeating things you have learned intellectually. In the case of the first century disciples, they were not just parroting what they had heard, but they were ministering truth that had become a vital part of their lives.

As with the singing parrot, the other side of the coin applies. We can mimic another person's reality and never discover our own creative expression. Even though we can learn from the experiences of others, each of us must live out our own authentic existence. With the exception of being like Christ, we mustn't try to be like anyone but ourselves. Otherwise, we undermine our God-given gift of individuality.

Things to Consider

People called to impact their culture can't afford to live in the shadow of another person's experience. There must be an awareness that a piece of God's character and nature is given to each and every person on Earth. Otherwise, we limit the way that the Creator chooses to manifest His diverse creativity to a world that is overrun with a mentality of sameness.

The prophet Elijah found this to be true while visiting the sacred mountain where Moses had earlier encountered God in an earthquake, wind, and fire. As seen in 1 Kings 19:11-13, the Lord did not manifest Himself to Elijah in these ways, but rather revealed Himself through a still, small voice. The irony was astounding. Both prophets encountered the *same* God on the *same* mountain, but each of them experienced a different aspect of God's person.

The point is that we cannot find our connection with God on the mountain of another person's experience. Because of His creative genius, God often reveals Himself to us in diverse and extraordinary ways. The God behind the experience never changes, but the manner in which He expresses Himself varies from person to person and from generation to generation.

To put it bluntly, there are no guarantees for the fulfillment of a future that is based on another person's encounter with the supernatural. In order to find your authentic existence, you must discover who you are and how you relate to the diverse manifestations of the Creator. The first step of this journey begins the moment you embrace the unique way that God has chosen to reveal Himself through your life today.

6

Authentic Voice

"Individuality is God's gift to each of us.
What we do with that individuality
is our gift to humanity."

—Larry Randolph—

All things in Heaven and Earth are attracted to authenticity. As a conference speaker, I am constantly challenged to express myself in a manner that's authentic. Most of the time, I can tell by the response of a crowd whether I'm communicating from my heart or just mechanically dispensing information. The proof is in the positive way that humans recognize and respond to authentic signals sent by other human beings. For the most part, people are extremely attracted to authenticity and turned off by anything artificial.

This distinction applies to every area of life. Whether a salesperson, schoolteacher, public speaker, or minister, the challenge is learning to operate in the "authenticity zone." It's being genuine that makes you believable and puts people at ease with who you are. Any successful salesperson knows that you must sell yourself before you can sell your product. People will believe what you're offering is real only if you are real.

In my line of work, I deal with people who are confused by this issue. There are two groups: The first group is made up of authentic people who are naturally spiritual. The second group consists of inauthentic people who copy others in order to appear spiritual. One group has learned to live out their God-given originality; the other group tries to live out the hopes and dreams of others.

In my opinion, the more annoying is the latter group who often confuse spiritual authenticity with religious imitations. Because they haven't discovered the value of being an original, they tend to mimic the mannerisms of other believers, hoping to compensate for a glaring lack of spirituality in their own lives. At first glance, their spirituality may look authentic, but all too often it's simply a bad imitation of the real thing.

Being an Original

The same scenario can also be found in other areas of life. In popular American culture, for example, there is a growing number of performers in the entertainment industry known as impersonators. Many of these impressionists are experts at imitating the appearance and mannerisms of movie stars and other celebrities, while others have learned to mimic the voice and songs of famous recording artists.

One reason these performers are able to imitate the traits and characteristics of other people is neurological by nature. Recent discoveries in the field of neuroscience suggest that many of them have unknowingly activated a system of "mirror neurons" in the frontal and parietal regions of the brain that enable them to accurately mimic the world around them. Somehow they have learned to access these specific neurons, which allow them to simulate the actions and behavior of those they observe. Basically, they have an inherent, biological knack for imitating the speech and mannerisms of other people.

No matter how great impersonators are at their jobs, though, one thing is certain: Like the pseudo-spiritual people I mentioned earlier, their material is simply a copy of an original and lacks the essence of authenticity. A friend of mine in the entertainment business suggested that they needed to "find their own groove." His musician's cliché simply meant to me, "Stop using your God-given creativity to imitate others and just be yourself."

Fortunately, this simple wisdom was a core value for many great leaders throughout history. The ultimate example is seen in the way Jesus of Nazareth embraced His own individuality nearly two thousand years ago. He clearly understood the importance of being an original and never let the opinion of the "politically correct" crowd influence the unique way that He conducted His life and ministry. On many occasions, He upset the social and theological etiquette of the religious elite by behaving in an unusual manner, performing bizarre miracles, and speaking in proverbs and riddles. He was truly an original thinker and never considered the possibility of mimicking the ministry style of others.

The same was true of other men in history, who at the risk of becoming social outcasts, demonstrated the very essence of originality. Because of his unorthodox thinking, the famous scientist Galileo encountered the wrath of the Medieval Church in the 1600s by suggesting that the earth is round, not flat. Misunderstood and persecuted by the religious establishment, he was isolated from mainstream society and lived as a misfit in the world.

Several decades earlier, Martin Luther, the great spiritual reformer also offended the Church of his day with a forward-thinking theology that was refreshingly different from traditional orthodoxy. Because he exhibited the courage to be an authentic voice, he was widely criticized by the status quo of his day. He, too, was rejected and eventually persecuted by many of the religious elite.

Like other original thinkers, all of these men were living proof that intellectual and spiritual authenticity is frequently incompatible with religious dogma. As history reveals, any form of originality that appears to be a threat to the belief system of its day is often met with a flood of opposition. The English novelist William Somerset Maugham put it into perspective when he wrote:

> "The world in general doesn't know what to make
> of originality; it's startled out of its comfortable habits
> of thought, and its first reaction is one of anger."

Voice or Echo?

Recently, I was challenged about the issue of authenticity by another bird story. My wife told me about a woman who had two cats and a parrot. The cats slept under the lady's bed on the second story of her house, and the parrot lived in a cage outside the bedroom that overlooked the kitchen. Every morning before going to work she would call the cats downstairs to the kitchen to feed them breakfast.

> You were created to be a voice, not an echo.

One day, the woman decided to stay home from work and rest. After sleeping late into the morning, she was suddenly awakened by the whirring noise of an electric can opener and the whooshing sound of freshness that comes from a can being opened. To her amazement a voice that sounded like her own began to call, "Here, kitty, kitty! Here, kitty, kitty!" At that point, both cats ran out from under the bed and down the stairs into the kitchen expecting to be fed. After jumping out of bed to investigate the suspicious sounds, the lady discovered the playful parrot imitating the sound of the can opener and mimicking her voice. Needless to say, the cats were agitated by the fake call to breakfast.

After hearing the story, two things became apparent. First, I recognized that impersonations for the purpose of entertainment are exactly that—good entertainment. In fact, some of my favorite types of entertainers are comedians who have learned to access their mirror neurons and add impersonations to their comedic routine.

Regrettably, many great men and women who command pulpits, college podiums, political offices, and other public platforms can also be talented impersonators. Like the parrot, their identity is often defined by who they mimic rather than who they are. Because they haven't discovered their authentic voice, they are inclined to express the convictions of others and often give out empty and misleading information. Without realizing it, their life becomes an echo instead of a genuine voice with a genuine message.

In the early days of my ministry, I was equally guilty of imitating the ministry styles of other people. All too often, hungry people were attracted to what they believed was the sound of authenticity only to find an imitation of the real thing. Looking back, I now realize that my impersonations had a low impact on those I was called to influence and neutralized my ability to be myself.

With God's help, however, I have worked hard on this area and have committed myself to being authentic. I now realize that it takes courage to be myself in a society that celebrates sameness. I also understand that I've been given a unique gift of the Spirit, not the gift of impersonation. I have found that it's not only a privilege to be *me* in personality and gifting, but an absolute necessity.

I Want to Be Me!

One of the greatest challenges in life is to be an original in a world overrun with impersonators. Although you can admire others, you must be careful not to imitate their mannerisms and personalities.

William Shakespeare gave it a poetic touch when he said, "God has given you one face and you make yourself another." The underlying implication is that the world needs the original breath you have to offer, not an imitation of another person. Honestly, if God had wanted you to be like someone else, He would have made you someone else.

Based on this reality, it's important to recognize your own value and unearth the originality that lies deep within your being. Special attention must be given to the inner voice of your soul that cries out, "I want to be me!" Actually, there must be a total abandonment of anything that limits your ability to be yourself. Otherwise, you will spend your life dreaming about the greatness of others, instead of living out your own authentic existence.

Sadly, some of my most valued friends, though incredibly gifted, struggle with this issue. Intellectually, they understand the significance of authenticity, but much of their time is spent trying to live vicariously through the accomplishments of famous preachers throughout history. They are mesmerized by the gifting of others and often pour themselves into sermons and writings of celebrated ministers of the past. Their great hope is to receive a piece of yesterday's glory.

Certainly, I appreciate the extraordinary gifting of spiritual pioneers and cannot overstate the priceless value of truth that's passed from generation to generation. However, we must not abandon our own God-given purpose in pursuit of gifting that belonged to great men and women throughout history. Their ministries were designed to function perfectly in their own generation, but when taken out of historical context, they have less impact on today's culture.

Living Your Authentic Life

In life's journey, we must all embrace what God is doing in us today. That means our purpose in life must be relevant to the time and culture in which we live. Although we should respect yesterday and have a vibrant hope for the future, we are called to live in the present, not the past. In fact, it's foolish to think we can replicate the experiences of others and expect to find our own threshold of authenticity.

Does this mean that we completely disconnect from the past?

Certainly not! It's a great privilege to incorporate yesterday's truth into our spiritual foundation. But honestly, we will never reach our destination by looking in the rearview mirror of life.

> It takes great courage to be yourself.

Instead of trying to recapture yesterday's reality, we must ask God to help us find our authentic voice today. In every aspect of life, we must ask Him for the grace to be ourselves.

For the most part, this process is not easy and it will not happen overnight. Realistically, your path to authenticity is filled with many twists and turns, and it usually takes a lifetime to make the shift from being an impersonator to living an authentic life. The risks are often challenging and will most likely take you outside of your comfort zone. But when your passion to be *you* becomes greater than your temptation to mimic others, you will experience the joy of a unique existence.

To assist you in your journey, I want to offer a few pointers that are simple but powerful. Hopefully, these truths will help you find your authentic life and will enable you to navigate through the ideology of sameness that is rampant throughout much of the world today:

- Be yourself at all times and in all places.
- Be true to your inner convictions.
- Accept your individual uniqueness.
- Don't be intimidated by the critique of the status quo.
- Never apologize for who you were created to be.
- Learn to trust your God-given instincts.
- Don't fear those who misunderstand your uniqueness.
- Be content with your individuality.
- Don't try to live another person's reality.
- Make up your mind to be real and genuine.
- Don't compare yourself with others.
- Protect your originality at all cost.
- Never downplay the importance of your creativity.
- Live in your own God-inspired reality.
- Avoid impersonations of someone else's life.
- Believe that you are one of a kind.
- Never underestimate the value of your individuality.
- Dare to be different.
- Be a voice, not an echo.
- Always be an original.

Things to Consider

By now, I hope it's sinking in that you should be yourself, not who others think you should be. It's time to fully embrace your individual uniqueness and resist any expression of your life and spirituality that may seem disingenuous. Keep in mind that most people are attracted to authenticity and are turned off by imitations. For this reason, your call to live an authentic life must begin with the decision to be an original.

That's why my primary motivation in this section was to encourage you to recognize your own uniqueness and become the person God created you to be. When you pursue someone else's dream rather than living out your own passion, it can threaten the fulfillment of your destiny. Just as Esau forfeited his birthright to his brother, Jacob, in Genesis 25:31, there's a risk of losing your God-given inheritance and ultimately your unique place in history.

Then again, if you have already embraced your individuality but you're not sure how to receive the spiritual gifts that are available to you, the following chapter will be helpful. After all, it's very important for these God-breathed gifts to be identified, uncovered, and incorporated into your life.

7

Authentic Gifting

"To the same degree that you are called to live an authentic life, you have been endowed with extraordinary gifting."

—Larry Randolph—

One of the most incredible concepts in the Bible has to do with the diversity of gifts and talents given to mankind. Some of these gifts are present at birth. Other gifting is offered by the Holy Spirit after our conversion to Christ. In either case, there is a unique God-deposit in humanity that's available to anyone willing to reach out for their full endowment.

In a powerful declaration to the church at Ephesus, Paul gives considerable attention to this issue. He strongly insists in Ephesians 4:7 that every person has been given a divine gift, according to the generosity of Christ. As I will deal with later, Paul describes these gifts and their distinctive nature in his writings to the Romans and Corinthians, stating, "There are varieties of gifts, but the same Spirit." Peter also addresses this reality in 1 Peter 4:10, instructing those who receive these gifts to utilize them to serve others—as good stewards of God's abundant grace.

These extraordinary verses tell us several things about the nature of God-given gifts. Both apostles make it clear that we've been given an inheritance from Heaven. There are no exceptions or exclusions—meaning no one is left out of the distribution process. The conclusion is that all of us, no matter how carnal or spiritual, possess within ourselves a treasure chest of spiritual gifts that waits to be discovered.

A failure to recognize and embrace these gifts, however, can greatly jeopardize our potential for success. Like a ship without a sail, a lack of understanding about divine gifting can keep us from going where the winds of Heaven desire us to go. Thus, the presence of "spiritual gifts" in our lives not only enables us to live a purposeful life today, but plays an important role in the fulfillment of our future destiny.

To experience the full impact of this reality, it's important to understand the nature of these gifts and the manner in which they are distributed. By definition, theologians tell us that the English word *gift* in the New Testament comes from the Greek word *charisma*, which means a "free endowment" or "divine gratuity." In contemporary terms, it's what our culture refers to as being gratuitous—such as giving a tip at a restaurant.

In either context the message is the same. The simple beauty of "charisma gifting" is that we have been given something that costs us absolutely nothing. At no time can we earn this privilege, nor can we make ourselves worthy enough to deserve these complimentary gifts. They come courtesy of Heaven and are a loving expression of Christ's generosity.

All we have to do is receive them!

Receiving Your Gifts

In terms of receiving spiritual gifts, there are several things we need to understand. Throughout the New Testament, we are warned about an indifferent attitude toward our spiritual endowment. In Matthew 7:7, for example, we are admonished to be persistent when petitioning God for the gifts of the Holy Spirit. In keeping with this admonition, Paul strongly states in 1 Corinthians 14:1 that it's not an option, but a command of the Spirit to "desire spiritual gifts."

In order to follow these directives, it's helpful to recognize the difference between the Greek and English meanings of the phrase "desire spiritual gifts." First of all, the English word *desire,* which is related to the word *wish,* means to hope or long for something in an emotional sense. In contrast, the Greek word *zello,* from which the English word *desire* is translated, means "to be zealous for" and "to covet earnestly." Unlike the passive inflection of the English word *desire,* the Greek word *zello* is an action word that implies passionate pursuit. That's why many Bible teachers tell us that Paul's command to "desire spiritual gifts" could have been loosely translated, "Pursue and run after spiritual gifts."

As mentioned earlier, the apostle Peter also instructs us to "receive spiritual gifts." Once again, the English word *receive* is passive, and much like the word *desire,* it implies an emotional and mental response that is independent of action. Yet the Greek word *lambano,* from which the English word *receive* is translated, denotes a sense of assertiveness and literally means "to take hold of" and "seize by force." Perhaps this explains the often misunderstood Scripture in Matthew 11:12 that says the Kingdom of Heaven is apprehended by those who aggressively seize their inheritance by force.

Considering the importance of this truth, I find it extremely naive to just "wait on the Lord" as many teach—hoping for the moment that God will step down from His throne to activate our gifts. The more I study Scripture, the more I believe we need to recognize the value of our heavenly inheritance and unearth the treasures we've been given. With the passing of every day, I'm increasingly convinced of our responsibility to persistently knock on Heaven's door until we are fully endowed with our spiritual gifts.

How long will it take to embrace these endowments and cultivate our individual gifts?

> God has placed extraordinary gifts in our lives, hoping we will discover them.

I'm not sure—it varies from person to person. But as you can see, there's a lot more to receiving your inheritance than just acknowledging the presence of spiritual gifting. Although they cost you nothing, you must pursue these gifts with an attitude of relentless determination. I know it's somewhat of a paradox, but only a passionate, aggressive pursuit will bring you face to face with the reality of your endowment. Quite simply, you must lay aside all timidity and false humility and seize your spiritual birthright—now, not later.

Christmas Every Day

The concept of pursuing spiritual gifts was made real to me several years ago. It was Christmas Eve and I was waiting on the front porch for my grandchildren to arrive for dinner. After the traditional holiday meal, my plan was to sit down in the family room and open presents. I had somehow envisioned a quiet, peaceful evening of Christmas cheer that was spirited but controllable.

To my amusement, however, the car arrived with overly excited grandkids bouncing up and down in their seats. Filled with anticipation, they jumped out of the backseat and dashed through the front door where the presents were waiting under the Christmas tree. The atmosphere was no longer calm and cozy as I had imagined but was charged with the buzz of youthful expectation.

For several blessed seconds, everything seemed to be under control. Then, in sheer delight, one of my grandsons plunged under the tree, tearing into the presents, yelling and screaming like an Apache warrior. He had no regard for the names on the packages or the attractive wrapping. He just wanted to find his gift—and if that meant opening every present under the tree, then so be it! Oblivious to the loud protest of his mother, he continued in his blind pursuit of happiness, showing no signs of shyness.

As you would expect, my first reaction was to correct him for breaking Christmas protocol. As I mentioned, our family tradition was to first share a meal and then to distribute the presents in an orderly manner. But after seeing the look of joyful excitement on his face, I was totally disarmed by his youthful enthusiasm. Then deep inside my soul a voice said, "This is what it's all about—the joy of receiving what's been freely given to you." At that point, I said to the rest of the grandkids, "Go ahead! Go for it! Don't wait on us."

As I watched the wonderful chaos that followed, something extraordinary began to unfold in my heart. I caught a glimpse of how this gift thing works in the Kingdom of God. Every day is Christmas in our heavenly Father's house. The Lord has placed extraordinary gifts under the Tree of Life with hopeful expectation that we will discover them.

Furthermore, we don't need a dream or vision to instruct us on how and when to receive, nor do we need an angel to bump us on the head. All we need is to shake off the timidity that holds us captive and unashamedly dive under the tree. If in the excitement we open the wrong gift—then that's alright. Our heavenly Father loves us and will sort it out in due time. Better yet, He might give us our heart's desire.

That day, I learned that you can never err on the side of expectation. There is nothing wrong with eager anticipation and everything right about a childlike innocence to pursue your wildest spiritual desires. Jesus highlighted this truth when He said, "Unless you become like little children, you will not enter the Kingdom of Heaven." He also told His followers that if they would continue to bear fruit, they could ask anything in His Father's name and He would give it to them.

Uniquely Gifted

Another thing I noticed that day was the significance that each personalized gift brought to every child. It seemed as though my grandchildren understood the thoughtfulness that went into the selection of each present and the love it represented to them as individuals. Needless to say, their self-esteem was boosted by a unique gift that was totally different from all the others.

In much the same way, every one of us has been given a personalized gift from God. As mentioned earlier, these gifts are His "love language" and reflect the Lord's affection for every person in His family. What's more, considerable thought has gone into the selection of these gifts and the potential impact they can have on our lives. They are expressions of Heaven's generosity that come straight from the heart of our heavenly Father.

Also, these "free endowments" are unique to the life of each and every believer. The diversity of gifts referred to in Paul's letter to the Corinthian church tells us they are distinctive in nature, quality, amount, and form. And because of the variety of these gifts, no two people express them in exactly the same way. Your gift may be similar to another person's gift, but it will differ in the way it's revealed through your individual personality. This shows us that diversity speaks many different languages and is a perfect sounding board for the diverse personality of God.

That's why, in recognizing and appreciating each and every gift, we come to see a more complete picture of the Creator's heart. On the other hand, a decline in diversity of gifting will lead to a decline in the understanding of His person. If you take away one single gift from a person's life, for instance, you lose a piece of the Lord's character reflected through humanity. In time, the absence of that gift will jeopardize the overall color of God's Kingdom on Earth. It would be like taking purple out of the rainbow or the string section from an orchestra.

> If you take away one single gift from a person's life, you lose a piece of God's character that's reflected through humanity.

Inspired Gifting

At this point, it's necessary to address one of the most important questions regarding our spiritual inheritance. What are the distinguishing characteristics of these divine gifts that Paul wrote about and how are they expressed through a person's life?

Contrary to the opinion of many Bible scholars today, the benevolence of God provides us with a vast supply of gifts that are relevant to modern society. The most well known are the nine "charisma" gifts listed in 1 Corinthians 12:7-10. These gifts are entirely supernatural, and as mentioned earlier, they are distributed by the person of the Holy Spirit. Included in this list are the gifts of healing, prophecy, and miracles, along with six other expressions of supernatural power.

There is also an assortment of other gifts found in Romans 12:6-8. They consist of exhortation, hospitality, giving, mercy, and various other endowments. In addition, Paul lists five administrative gifts in Ephesians 4:11 that are given to lead the universal Church. They include the offices of apostle, prophet, evangelist, pastor, and teacher.

Then there are the more artistic gifts seen in the lives of people throughout the Old Testament. One of the most striking is the poetic brilliance of Solomon. *Easton's Bible Dictionary* tells us this legendary king created approximately three thousand stories and proverbs and composed more than one thousand songs. His father, David, was also a renowned poet and possessed one of the most extraordinary musical gifts found in biblical history. As stated by the *International Standard Bible Encyclopedia,* this gifted harpist and lyricist composed volumes of sacred poetry and invented many of the instruments used in the Old Testament temple. Another good example is Miriam's expression of celebratory worship in Exodus 15:20, which could have been David's inspiration for choreographing much of the temple worship in 2 Chronicles 8:14.

Other biblical characters, although different in gifting, possessed divine endowments that enabled them to excel in the political arena of their day. Daniel, for example, quickly rose to the rank of governor of Babylon because of his amazing gifting as a visionary and interpreter of dreams. Also remarkable was Joseph's gift of dream interpretation, which took him from the disgrace of prison to the prestige of Pharaoh's throne, where he served as chief ruler in Egypt (Daniel 2; Genesis 40 - 41).

Unique Gift-mix

As you can see, there are many examples of divine gifting revealed in the lives of Bible characters throughout history. Even so, it's small thinking to limit these gifts to such a select group of people. Today's generation also possess many gifts and talents that the scientific community has only recently begun to recognize. Thanks to the extensive research and advancement of modern science, we have a more complete picture of the complex gift-mix that's resident in all of humanity. We now understand, in part, the beauty of the human soul and the way our gifting is expressed through our intellectual, emotional, and spiritual temperaments.

Also of great importance to this issue is the groundbreaking research in the 1960s that led to the discovery of left-brain and right-brain thinking. The conclusion of leading neuroscientists was that the left side of the brain is mostly logical and analytical, while the right side of the brain is intuitive and creative. The assumption was that these two hemispheres of the brain provide us with a unique neurological profile that shapes our existence and influences the way our gifting is processed and expressed.

Some of the defining characteristics of right-brain and left-brain thinkers are:

Left Brain

- Analytical thinking (attention to detail, task-oriented, systematic, orderly processing)

- Linguistic thinking (verbal processing, logical reasoning)

- Objective thinking (intentional, extensive planning)

- Rational thinking (common sense, logical processing)

- Box thinking (methodical, black-and-white processing)

- Linear thinking (sequential, systematically progressive)

Right Brain

- Metaphorical thinking (abstract, allegorical perspective)
- Aural thinking (processing sound)
- Abstract thinking (conceptual, mystical, unpredictable)
- Spatial thinking (intuitive, perceptual, visual processing)
- Circular thinking (repetitive, creative, lots of options)
- Intuitive thinking (gut reactions, acute sensitivity)

Now combine these unique characteristics of the brain with the distinct personality and emotional makeup of each person, and the possibilities are endless. Out of this gift-mix comes musicians, athletes, accountants, scientists, nurses, architects, philosophers, doctors, carpenters, politicians, poets, actors, computer programmers, and a never-ending list of people who contribute to the growth and expansion of society.

And when you add the biblical gifts of mercy, healing, administration, prophecy, and other spiritual endowments to the mix, you have an even greater number of mind-boggling possibilities. The end product is a blend of natural talents and spiritual gifts that together give us a better picture of how God intended the human race to function.

Things to Consider

Considering the infinite possibilities of our gift-mix, it truly does take all kinds of people (with all kinds of gifts) to make the world go 'round. That's why you should never compromise the originality of your gifting or allow others to impose on you what they have been called to be. If you do, you could end up living someone else's life.

What's more, once you have settled this issue, another critical dynamic comes into play. After embracing your God-given individuality, you must then confront the negative barriers in your path that block your potential for greatness. It is this positive approach that will enable you to live out your uniqueness in front of others.

Actually, it all comes down to finding the courage to deal with the limitations that restrict your forward motion in life. As I will address in the next few chapters, you must learn to maximize your shortcomings and push through the constraints that keep you from becoming the authentic person you were created to be.

PART
THREE

*Confronting Your
Constraints and Failures*

8

Breaking Through Your Constraints

"Twenty years from now you will be more disappointed by the things that you didn't do than by the ones you did do. So throw off the bowlines. Sail away from the safe harbor. Catch the trade-winds in your sail. Explore, dream, discover..."

—Mark Twain—
American humorist, writer, and lecturer

One of my greatest worries as a teenager was that I would grow old and never become what I was created to be. I was deeply troubled by the possibility that my life could end without finding my God-given purpose. Many nights I lay awake for hours at a time, fretting about my future and trying to figure out how I could get to where I was meant to be in life.

Even more challenging was the discovery as a young adult that I had a personal role in the development of my destiny. I was in my mid-twenties before I realized that I alone had the power either to resist or embrace the Creator's design for my existence. Fortunately, I accepted the challenge to co-labor with Heaven in the shaping of my destiny, and things began to change. With God's help, I made a decision to close the door on passivity and began to maximize my potential with a more positive approach to life.

The result was remarkable! I immediately discovered that an extraordinary future requires extraordinary risk. I found that new territory is never taken by passive people, but by those willing to risk it all on their passion in life. Knowing this, I was determined to take bold steps to overcome the obstacles that stood between me and my potential destiny. The choice was mine alone. I could press forward in the direction of my hopes and dreams—or settle for a mundane existence and miss the life that I was destined to live.

> New territory is never taken by passive people, but by those willing to risk it all on their passion in life.

Armed with this truth, I began a passionate search to discover my purpose in life. I studied the Bible extensively and consumed a great number of books and commentaries about God and religion. Driven for significance, I fasted and prayed for days at a time. On one occasion, I drank nothing but water for seven days as I searched for purpose and spiritual inspiration.

Looking for Adventure

To the shock of my Christian friends, I also began to look for inspiration in secular venues. In fact, I was greatly inspired by the song "Born to Be Wild" by Steppenwolf. Although the message was somewhat radical, it revealed the passionate desire of a young generation to experience all that life had to offer. Every time I heard this song, something deep inside my soul shouted, "that's me!" In a mysterious way, I was intensely moved by the songwriter's longing for meaning and adventure in the following lyrics:

"Get your motor runnin'

Head out on the highway

Lookin' for adventure

And whatever comes our way

Yeah, darlin', go make it happen

Take the world in a love embrace

Fire all of your guns at once

Explode into space

Like a true nature's child

We were born, born to be wild

We can climb so high

I never wanna die

Born to be wild

Born to be wild."

Why would God use such an edgy song to stir my passion for adventure?

I'm not sure, but contrary to what some may believe, I clearly heard a call to destiny in the explosive lyrics. Of course, I didn't think my generation was born to be wild in a destructive sense; nor did I endorse the reckless lifestyle of the rock 'n' roll culture. But like the words of this legendary song, I did believe we were born for outrageous adventures in life. In my young mind, anything less than total abandonment to a life filled with significance was a complete waste of time.

The same value for significance and adventure is still alive in my heart today. Although several decades have passed since my youthful pursuit for meaning, I'm convinced more than ever of my need to live a purpose-driven life. I am deeply aware of the possibility that I can miss my connection with destiny because of an attitude of indifference.

To be honest, the older I get, the more I am determined to maximize my life purpose and push the limits of my potential. I suspect that any disregard for this pursuit of adventure will haunt my generation in our twilight years. When we have an opportunity to review the sum of our lives on Earth, many of us will be sad for selling ourselves short—for not believing in the possibility of what we could have been. The regrets will be great for those who never lived out their dreams or fully embraced their purpose in life. Maybe that's why Revelation 21:4 says that God will have to wipe the tears from our eyes when we get to Heaven.

Confronting Your Constraints

Helen Keller once said, "Life is either a daring adventure or nothing."

I couldn't agree more. For me, that translates, "Accept no imitations or limitations in life." Cast off the constraints that limits your capacity to live big. Take a risk! Be daring! And for crying out loud, don't miss your chance at success by clinging to familiar ground.

Every notable person understands this challenge. Whether they are a successful artist, athlete, or businessperson, the difference between them and most others is their proactive approach to life. It's not luck or fate that brings them success, but a willingness to take risks in order to become what they always wanted to be. Most of them entertain no boundaries and refuse to be intimidated by the fear factor. They dare to defy the threatening voices in the world and often do what the cynics say they can't do.

Others who play it safe rarely lead successful lives. Paralyzed by the fear of failure, they shrink back from every opportunity for success, hiding behind a mentality of defeatism. Because of an overwhelming sense of despair that comes from the negative fallout of their past, they lose hope and have little heart for daring adventures in life. They have yet to learn that their passion to succeed must be greater than the limitations they were born with or the personal constraints they acquire over time.

I, too, had to deal with this issue as a young man growing up in the Deep South. The moment my feet hit the floor, I seemed to be running against the winds of opposition. Born into extreme poverty in rural Arkansas, I had very little self-esteem and was limited by a heart murmur and the crippling effects of Rheumatic Fever. I was extremely introverted, filled with fear, and often breathless from anxiety. Except for the times my father put me in the pulpit to sing, I couldn't look people in their eyes or speak to them without trembling hands and a shaking voice. By most standards, I was the least likely to succeed at anything.

Ironically, though, I always sensed the calling to lead a life of adventure. In spite of being raised in the exact opposite atmosphere, I knew God would one day help me break through the limitations of my upbringing. Even though the odds were stacked against me and the roadblocks were many, I was determined to find a positive environment that would be helpful to my success.

Once I accepted the calling as a young man to be a pastor, I had to confront the underprivileged mentality that came from being raised in an atmosphere steeped in negative thinking. Years later, when I began to travel as a conference speaker, I also had to overcome the paralyzing fear of speaking in front of large crowds. And in order to maintain my busy schedule, I had no choice but to deal with my irrational fear of flying.

As for writing, the limitations seemed even greater. When I attempted my first book, I didn't own a computer and wrote the manuscript in longhand in a spiral notebook. After editing with scissors and Scotch tape, I pieced the final product together and made copies for a few friends to read. Several of them never responded; others encouraged me to keep trying. One brave friend finally told me it was the worst piece of literature ever written.

Instead of shrinking back in rejection, I took a deep breath and started over. Although I possessed more passion than talent, I refused to be intimidated by my limitations. Again and again, I kept trying—pushing the boundaries of my skill and patience. I was acutely aware that I had to take advantage of every opportunity for success or face a bleak future. Driven by a passion to succeed, persistence became the tipping point for breakthrough. Eventually the book was published and is still in print today.

All of these experiences have taught me that I'm capable of overcoming extreme limitations. Early in life, I realized that I would never live a turnkey existence and had to boldly confront the personal constraints that held me captive. I have dreamed big, dared to take risks, and blindly pushed through circumstances and situations that seemed impossible. And while my accomplishments are small when compared to other people, I am thankful I've made it this far. With God's help, I have defied the odds and even surprised myself, now and then.

Just recently, while thinking about slowing down, I heard the Spirit whisper to my heart, "If you want to stop, it's alright. You have already gone beyond your potential for success and have greatly exceeded our expectations up here."

At last, I thought, *a voice of reason that will shelter me from the performance mentality that often sneaks up on people struggling to press through their personal constraints.*

Breakdown or Breakthrough?

As we will see in the next few chapters, there are many ways to harness your potential and overcome seemingly impossible barriers. Some of these breakthroughs are easy to accomplish. Others are more difficult and require a lot of inner-strength and determination.

No matter what difficulty you face, the most critical aspect of breakthrough is to never stop pushing forward. Often, your greatest breakthrough is only one push beyond your greatest resistance. All you need is passion along with a determination to defy the devil if necessary. As Winston Churchill once said, "If you're going through hell, keep going."

One good example of breakthrough is seen in the dynamics of flight. According to the fundamental laws of aviation, an aircraft must defy the natural laws of gravity in order to fly. Because gravity and lift are opposing forces, as are drag and thrust, there must be a reversal of these principles for flight to actually occur.

For an aircraft to experience maximum lift upon takeoff, for example, the force of thrust must be greater than the force of drag and the downward force of gravity. Without achieving proper thrust and lift, the plane is simply unable to leave the ground. Conversely, when the plane's thrust and lift exceed the force of gravity, the aircraft becomes airborne. The shuddering and shaking that occurs during takeoff is the plane breaking the laws of nature that try to hold it earthbound.

What would happen if the plane didn't reach maximum thrust and lift at the end of the runway? What if the pilot reduced the engine power because of the extreme resistance at the point of takeoff?

There are two choices: Give up or go forward. Break down or break through. If the pilot is intimidated by the laws of gravity, the result will be less than favorable. Both the aircraft and the pilot will be at extreme risk. Then again, if the pilot pushes through the resistance, the plane will mount up to the heavens as a testimony to the triumph of lift and thrust over gravity. Once the aircraft is completely airborne and levels out in flight, the more aerodynamic it becomes. When cruising altitude is finally achieved, the airplane is able to fly with minimal thrust.

The same is true of a jet traveling from subsonic to supersonic speed. This transition in flight, known as breaking the sound barrier, is met with great resistance. At the point when an aircraft approaches the speed of sound, there is a resistance buildup around the plane known as shock waves. These shock waves create a wake drag that alters the aerodynamic forces of the jet, causing considerable vibration of the wings. Often the controls of the plane will become buried in the wake and are rendered ineffective.

At this critical juncture, the pilot must make a decision to back off or push through the barrier. If the plane's speed is reduced significantly, the turbulence from the shock wave begins to smooth out and the flight returns to normal. If the pilot accelerates the plane beyond the speed of sound, however, the shock wave moves to the rear of the aircraft and the adverse effect on the wings is no longer a problem.

At this point, the effects are astonishing! The outcome is a sonic boom that announces the jet has punched through the sound barrier. In defiance of natural laws, the aircraft is now able to fly at supersonic speed with little resistance.

Moving Forward

As with the dynamics of flight, there are opposing forces at work that want to keep you earthbound. All the same, you must make a decision to fly—to go full throttle until you feel the lift of God's Spirit under your wings. If you don't, you will lose your nerve and eventually your momentum. If you hesitate and look back to the past, like Lot's wife in Genesis 19:26, you could severely jeopardize your moment of transition.

To experience complete breakthrough, it's necessary to sever the emotional and physical constraints that hold you back. Regardless of the difficulty, you must push through the barriers of poverty, abuse, low self-esteem, lack of education, and other negative factors I've already talked about. Whatever it takes, find a way to overcome the wind drag that holds your hopes and dreams captive, preventing you from soaring in life. Most of all, never let the difficulties of your past dictate the success of your future.

> Your greatest breakthrough is often one push beyond your greatest resistance.

Of course, that's easier said than done. But I'm speaking from personal experience, not from principle alone. In fact, I clearly remember the day that I closed my eyes to the adverse circumstances around me and decided to "make my move" in life. It wasn't easy, and I'm still not totally free from the shock waves of my past. However, I'm moving forward and have learned some extremely valuable lessons about the process of breaking through my constraints.

First, I have learned that people are limited only by the constraints they are afraid to confront. I've also found that if you're not standing at the extreme edge of purpose, you're probably taking up too much room. So take a risk and jump.

Get out of your box of confinement and dare to live in the possibility zone! You might find out that success is just one courageous leap away.

So, if you're thinking that you have somehow missed your chance, let me encourage you that it's never too late to be the person you are created to be. All you need is God's help and a fearless determination to break through to the other side of your personal constraints. Once there, you will look back and see that the most difficult part was finding the courage to take that first step.

Since your journey in life begins with the decision to move forward, I have put together a list to help jumpstart your breakthrough process:

- Pray that God will show you the issues that hold you back. Honesty is the first step to total breakthrough.

- Get rid of a reluctant attitude. Procrastination is your greatest threat to freedom.

- Forget about your past limitations. With God's help, your tomorrow can be greater than your yesterday.

- Don't treat your personal constraints as impossible barriers but as temporary obstacles.

- Push hard against your restraints. Your forward thrust must be greater than the resistance around you.

- Never give in to despair. Hopelessness will jeopardize your opportunity to lead a full life.

- Ruthlessly confront your limitations. Treat them as enemies to your destiny.

- Take responsibility for your life. Denial and self-pity will keep you from dealing with your limitations.

- Make a list of your constraints and limitations so you can begin to confront them one by one.

- Don't give up when there's no immediate response. Keep pushing through!

- Disclose your weaknesses to trustworthy friends who can support you in the breakthrough process.

- Get professional help if your constraints are too much for you and your friends to handle.

Things to Consider

To experience total breakthrough, you must never fear the process of transition. Like a caterpillar that becomes a butterfly, it's necessary to break through the cocoon that restricts your movement, preventing you from flying.

Paul clearly illustrates this analogy in Philippians 3:13-14, instructing us to forget those things that lie behind us, reaching forward to the upward call of God in Christ. He also implied in 2 Corinthians 5:17 that to reach this ultimate destiny, your old life must be put aside in order for new life to begin. Only then is it possible to be transformed into the image of Christ and to push through the restraints that keep you earthbound.

Will this process be difficult? Will you stumble in your quest to become what you are meant to be? Possibly, but do it anyway. It's never too late to make the daring leap from a life of constraints to a future without limits. And if you don't know how to make the proper transition, don't panic—God is more than willing to guide you.

Keep in mind that trained experts navigated the Titanic, while an amateur sailed Noah's Ark.

CHAPTER

9

Maximizing
Your Mistakes

*"When God created your destiny, He factored your
mistakes and blunders into the equation."*

—Larry Randolph—

For people desiring to live an extraordinary life, two things are certain—the opportunity for success and the probability of failure. The first will require your best effort to push forward in life. The latter will try your patience and test the integrity of your character. The eighteenth century writer John Homer Miller put it best when he wrote, "Your living is determined not so much by what life brings to you, but by the attitude you bring to life."

On some level, every person must deal with this reality. For many, success will always be an option, despite the ever-present threat of failure. For others, the very thought of failure is a dream-killer that neutralizes their forward motion in life. Because of the potential blunders and mistakes that await them on their journey, they often give up before they try. They are unaware that no risk brings no reward.

For those willing to take risks, though, there is good news. I've learned that failure (for the most part) isn't necessarily a bad thing. I'm also convinced that a life spent making mistakes is far better than a life spent doing nothing at all. That being the case, failing doesn't make you a failure; never trying makes you a failure.

Based on this reality, it's important that you recognize the opportunity in every difficulty. By definition, success is not measured by the absence of failure, but by the way you deal with failure. That being the case, it's not necessary to sanitize your life of all mistakes and blunders or make unnecessary excuses for your humanity. All you need is a bit of confidence and the courage to try again and again if necessary.

Even when things seem impossible, you must put your best foot forward and boldly confront the fear barrier that threatens your forward motion. I'm not suggesting that your failure ratio will instantly decrease. But if your passion to succeed is greater than your fear of failing, you will eventually learn to maximize your mistakes and get it right.

The lesson is unmistakably clear. You can serve failure or failure can serve you. If the first is true, fear will imprison your hopes and dreams for a prosperous future. Crippled by the fear of failure, you will drift through life never feeling the sting of defeat or the joy of success. Your path will certainly be safe from misfortune and danger, but your reward at the end of the journey will be disappointing.

Then again, if failure becomes your servant instead of your master, you will begin to see the fulfillment of your wildest dreams. Certainly, you will encounter many difficulties in your journey, and you might fail more than you ever envisioned. Even so, you will discover that failure is not the result of falling down but refusing to get up again. In time, you will learn not to be intimidated by the fear factor and will find that the harder you fall, the higher you will bounce. Even if you do fall on your face, at least you are falling forward.

I'm not suggesting that a positive mindset is all that is needed to achieve success, but once you develop this level of optimism, the possibilities are endless. Who knows? Your next failure could be the stepping-stone to your greatest success. You could be the next famous politician, musician, or scientist. In fact, you might surprise everyone and do the very thing people think you are incapable of doing. Better yet, you could fulfill your childhood dreams of greatness and go down in history as a person who succeeded against all odds.

> Your next failure could be the stepping-stone to your greatest achievement.

Again, the challenge is learning how to disempower your disappointments. By failing gracefully and capitalizing on your mistakes, you will maximize your potential for success. And if you keep falling forward and don't give in to discouragement, you will eventually reach your destiny in life. The payoff at the end of the journey will be far greater than anything you ever dreamed or imagined.

The Beauty of Mistakes

Robert F. Kennedy once said, "Only those who dare to fail greatly can achieve greatly." To put it another way, failing is the natural consequence of trying.

This truth was made real to me by my friend Graham Cooke. Several years ago, he was engaged in a time of prayerful meditation, hoping to hear from God. Although Graham was anticipating a long, drawn-out session, he had barely settled into a contemplative state of prayer when the Lord confronted him with an outrageous statement: "I wish you had made more mistakes in your life."

Shocked, Graham replied, "Lord, why would you want me to make mistakes?"

The immediate reply was, "If you had made more mistakes, at least I would have known you were trying."

After hearing Graham's story, something wonderful began to happen in my heart. It was like finding the missing piece of a lifelong puzzle. For me, that missing piece said, "Try harder and expect to make a lot of mistakes. Let God know you are moving forward by the mess you make trying to get to where He has called you to go."

Does this mean we are to live an immature life, never taking accountability for our actions?

Certainly, most of us are doing our best to push forward in life, trying hard to become the people we are called to be. The problem, though, is that we don't believe God is comfortable with the mistakes we make along the way. This is really difficult for those of us raised in a conservative, religious environment. We have adopted a philosophy that requires us to try harder without recognizing that there is grace to fail in the process. Consequently, we often go through life holding our breath—stifled by a performance mentality that applauds success and has little appreciation for the value of mistakes.

In order to break free from this deceptive mindset and breathe freely, it's necessary to see your blunders from God's perspective. You must understand that any voice telling you there's no room for failure is not the voice of your heavenly Father. It's either the voice of a defiled conscience or the unforgiving dictates of religious dogma. In either case, if you listen to these misleading voices, they will jeopardize your potential to become the person you are meant to be.

That is why it's so important to ignore the disapproval of your critics and learn to fail without remorse. The irony is that once you have failed completely, the possibilities are endless. You are totally free! Free from a performance mentality. Free from the expectations and pressure to produce a perfect track record. And if you don't get bogged down in discouragement and beat yourself up, you'll find that success belongs to those who dare to fail the most.

A good example of this truth was modeled by the great baseball legend Babe Ruth. In the year that he broke the record for the most homeruns, he also broke the record for the most strikeouts. Time and again, he was willing to risk failure for a chance at success. He never looked for the perfect pitch—he just swung the bat! The result was an incredible .690 lifetime slugging average that has yet to be topped.

How important is this kind of optimism to the way you view your success in life?

Although you might never be another Babe Ruth, you can give yourself permission to pursue the goals in life that might seem impossible. Honestly, you cannot afford to wait for the right moment to be successful. You must take a chance and swing the bat over and over again until you connect with your destiny. Bear in mind the words of the late author and poet Struthers Burt:

> "Men are failures, not because they are stupid, but
> because they are not sufficiently impassioned."

Try, Try Again

Much credit can be given to Thomas Watson, the founder of IBM, who said, "The way to succeed is to double your failure rate." Even more credit goes to the famous inventor Thomas Edison for actually living out the reality of this quote. In a wonderful way, he was a fearless risk-taker who refused to be intimidated by his failures.

It all began in 1878, when Edison boldly announced to the world that he would invent an inexpensive electric light that would replace the gas light. Greatly ridiculed, Edison tried over ten thousand different experiments, which included more than fifteen thousand materials and two thousand tests to find the right filament. After nearly two years of exhausting work, he finally demonstrated the first incandescent light bulb on October 21, 1879.

Like many great men and women in history, Edison was a firm believer in the importance of failure. He understood that failure was simply the pathway to success. He was quoted as saying, "Many of life's failures are people who did not realize how close they were to success when they gave up." Speaking of his difficulty in perfecting the light bulb, the prolific inventor declared, "I have not failed. I've just found ten thousand ways that don't work!"

> Success belongs to those who are willing to fail the most.

This kind of optimism was largely responsible for many of the 1,093 patents Edison amassed in a wide range of fields. In addition to the light bulb, some of the most well-known patents were for mining technology, commercial batteries, telecommunications, sound recording, and motion pictures. He worked tirelessly on his inventions, failing over and over again until he got it right.

Once, while Edison was working on developing a better battery, a discouraged assistant suggested that they should quit after performing fifty thousand unsuccessful experiments. "You must be pretty downhearted with the lack of progress," the assistant declared. Again, Edison responded with overflowing optimism. "Downhearted?" he quickly replied. "We've made a lot of progress. At least we know fifty thousand things that won't work!" In the end, he developed a nickel-iron alkaline battery that became an industry standard, still in use today!

What if Edison had grown weary with his research on batteries and stopped at 49,999 experiments? What if he had given up on the light bulb after 9,999 tries?

Thank God that Edison recognized, as did Winston Churchill, that "success is going from failure to failure without losing your enthusiasm." Had this inventor let failure shut him down, the world as we know it would be quite different. We might still be reading by candlelight! There would be no wireless communication and no alkaline batteries to run the electronic devices we rely on today. Equally tragic would be the absence of the motion picture camera, which Edison pioneered and later synchronized with sound.

In every way, Edison's life and work are living illustrations of success through failure. He showed the world that it's a gross misconception to believe that you can succeed through success alone. Like other great innovators in history, he proved that the road to success is often paved with the experience and wisdom found in failure.

Things to Consider

Regarding human failure, the famous writer and playwright Oscar Wilde once said, "Experience is simply the name we give our mistakes." James Joyce, another influential writer put it into perspective when he wrote, "A man's errors are his portals of discovery."

Both quotes reveal the greatness that can come from your shortcomings. As with these men, you mustn't fear to make a blunder or miss the opportunity in your failures. It's not your mistakes that jeopardize your potential for success, but your inability to capitalize on them.

Am I suggesting that you take pride in failure? Should you revel in your faults and inadequacies?

Certainly, you must work hard to reduce your margin of error. On the other hand, making a mistake doesn't necessarily mean you're a failure. Nor does the reality of failure disqualify you from living out your God-given destiny. In fact, today's failures can shape the learning curve that enables you to live a better life tomorrow.

10

Finding Hope in Failure

"Failure is the perfect opportunity to experience the benevolent grace and kindness of God."

—Larry Randolph—

Richard H. Nelson, a pioneer in the energy industry, said, "Never let the failures of yesterday use up your chances for success today."

Several decades ago, while scanning the TV channels, I came across a riveting interview with a Catholic priest that put this quote in perspective. The topic of discussion was finding hope in failure. In great detail, the priest told a riveting story he had witnessed about a man's journey from failure to success.

As I remember the story, the priest and a select group of American clerics were invited to the Vatican for an audience with the Pope in the 1970s. Upon early arrival in Rome, the priest checked into a hotel and then decided to visit a neighboring cathedral to pray. While walking past a beggar outside the door of the church, he hesitated momentarily with a funny feeling deep in his gut. It seemed there was something strangely familiar about the grubby man.

The next day, when the priest returned for Early Morning Prayer, he decided to stop and greet the beggar. Overcome by curiosity he asked, "What is your name?"

The beggar replied, "My name is John Doe."

In disbelief the priest said, "Surely you are not the same John Doe who attended seminary with me more than twenty years ago in America?"

The beggar sadly answered, "Yes, I am! But I became bitter, dropped out of seminary, and moved to Rome. Eventually, my life went down the drain, and for the last few years I've been living on the streets, begging in front of this cathedral." Then in a broken voice the beggar pleaded, "Please remember me in your prayers."

Second Chances

Several days later, when it was time to visit the Pope, the priest could think of nothing but the beggar. When his turn came to greet the Holy Father, he whispered a short version of the beggar's story in his ear and said, "Remember the poor man in your prayers."

Surprisingly, the Pope replied, "Come for dinner tomorrow and bring the beggar with you."

That night, the priest searched for the beggar and found him at his usual spot in front of the church. He enthusiastically told him about the Holy Father's request and took the man to his hotel for a bath and something to eat. After eating, the priest prepared a place for the beggar to sleep and then laid out an extra pair of his own shoes and pants for the beggar to wear to dinner the next day.

The following evening, the priest and the beggar sat with the Pope eating a silent dinner. When the meal was over, the Pope broke the uncomfortable silence with a stunning request.

He asked the priest to leave the room and then turned to the beggar and said, "I want you to hear my confession."

Shocked, the beggar protested, "You don't understand. I can't hear your confession because I'm no longer a priest."

At that point the Pope looked him in the eye and said in a forceful tone of voice, "Once a priest, always a priest! Now I want you to hear my confession."

Having no choice, the beggar reluctantly heard the Pope's confession. After the Pope was finished, the beggar, now under severe conviction, fell to the floor weeping. Trembling like a leaf in the wind, he pleaded with the Pope to bless him and forgive his many sins.

When the beggar's confession was over, the Pope called the American priest back into the room and made another shocking statement. He said, "I want you to speak to the Father of the church where this man has been begging and tell him I said to make him a priest over the poor and the homeless."

That day, the priest and the beggar left the Vatican with a renewed sense of hope. The American priest immediately made an appointment with the Father of the neighboring cathedral and the beggar was put to work ministering to the homeless.

"To this day," the priest declared in the interview, "the beggar-turned-priest is still serving faithfully in that particular parish in Rome."

The Antidote for Failure

Like the beggar, many today have experienced a failure to launch. Crippled by the agony of their mistakes, they've simply forfeited their potential for success and are now living a low-impact life.

As revealed in the last chapter, the road to success is strewn with the shattered dreams of those who have given in to fear and disappointment. Intimidated by human weakness and the probability of failure, many people have had the wind knocked out of them and have given in to hopelessness. In their mind, it's all over—forever.

A classic example of this kind is seen in the life of one of the most celebrated apostles in Church history. His name was Peter. Throughout his mentorship with Jesus, he was enthusiastic, passionate, and at times exceptionally brave. Just hours before Jesus was taken hostage by a group of religious leaders, the zealous disciple blurted out that he would follow the Lord to the grave if necessary. Later that night, he had the chance to prove his loyalty and bravely defended his Master by cutting off the ear of the high priest's servant with a sword.

Yet when push came to shove, the darker side of humanity began to surface in the sincere but presumptuous disciple. After Jesus was captured and put on trial, Peter lingered behind in the crowd, cursing and denying that he ever knew Him. Even more disturbing, he stood on the distant horizon at the Lord's crucifixion the next day, afraid to acknowledge Him for fear of retaliation. In the end, Jesus died alone, betrayed by a friend that had vowed to follow Him anywhere (Matthew 26:35-75).

What a devastating blow to Peter's hopes for a successful future. In his mind, his life was over. All seemed to be lost. His weakness had cost him everything—including his friendship with the Person he loved the most. He hated himself, and the haunting voice in his head constantly reminded him that he was a loser, a coward, and a traitor. Totally disillusioned by his failures, the despairing disciple returned to his former trade as a fisherman.

Like many people today, though, Peter didn't have Heaven's perspective about his life. He was clueless as to God's design for his future and never suspected the coming visitation that would free him from the anguish of failure. It probably never crossed his mind that he'd be given a fresh start and would recover his destiny—much less go down in history as one of the great fathers of the Christian faith.

Yet everything was about to change for the distraught fisherman. Because of the Lord's great love for Peter, Jesus focused on his potential, not on his mistakes and failures. The Bible reveals in John 21 that the Resurrected Christ visited Peter's fishing expedition early one morning and commissioned him to nurture the fledgling Church that the Lord had left behind.

> You must focus on your potential, not on your mistakes and failures.

Undoubtedly, Peter was encouraged by such a gracious proposal and was able to take a fresh breath, knowing there was hope in failure. All he needed was forgiveness for his past mistakes and the permission to try again. On that day, the Lord gave him both.

Recovering from Catastrophic Failure

The same scenario is also seen in the lives of other great men throughout the Bible. King David, for example, failed in ways unbecoming for someone known as "a man after God's heart." As documented in the Old Testament, his shortcomings led to parental failure, leadership collapse, and an act of disobedience that cost the lives of seventy thousand men. In a moment of weakness, Israel's beloved psalmist also committed adultery with a beautiful woman named Bathsheba, and then orchestrated the death of her husband (2 Samuel 11, 13, 24).

Like Peter, perhaps David thought his sins were greater than God's ability to restore his broken life. Many were the nights he lay sleepless, agonizing over his shortcomings and failures. In a riveting psalm, he proclaimed, "I am weary with my crying; my throat is parched; my eyes fail while I wait for my God." In another psalm, he declared, "For my life is spent with sorrow and my years with sighing; my strength has failed because of my iniquity" (Psalm 69:3; 31:10).

In spite of the agony that gripped David's soul, something extraordinary was about to take place. There is evidence in the latter portion of the Psalms that the Lord had encouraged his broken heart. The psalmist began to discover that the Almighty lifts up those who are bowed down, heals the brokenhearted, and binds up their wounds. In a striking display of gratitude in Psalm 136, David declared more than twenty times that God's "mercy endures forever." From that point forward, the tone of the book of Psalms begins to shift dramatically from a sense of anguish to gratitude.

Although human in every aspect, David learned not to be intimidated by failure. Apparently, he came to the conclusion that great warriors don't give up after losing a battle, nor do God-appointed kings forfeit their positions of leadership because of their shortcomings. Regardless of his failures, he knew better than to relinquish his right to the throne or let human weakness determine the success of his future. He understood that the way to cope with failure is to be honest about your faults, repent, receive forgiveness, and try again. That attitude qualified him as a man after God's own heart.

Imperfectly Authentic

Like many great men in history, a number of people today have retreated from their true calling in life. Discouraged by past failure, they often live an existence that is out of step with their God-given destiny. Even so, failure to launch is not always terminal, nor does it jeopardize a person's chance for a brighter future. Failure simply provides the perfect opportunity to engage your ultimate purpose and is by default the end of things old and the beginning of things new.

The impact of this reality was experienced by many of Jesus' followers in the first century. After His death and resurrection the Lord comforted a number of men and women in a series of supernatural visitations, encouraging them to move forward in their divine calling. As He did with Peter, the Resurrected Christ revealed His glory to a former prostitute named Mary Magdalene and later demonstrated His divine power to an unbelieving disciple called Thomas. On another occasion, He breathed upon a room full of disillusioned disciples in the book of Acts, imparting to them the power of the Holy Spirit (John 20:11-30; Acts 2:2).

As you might suspect, this brings me to several important questions. To what degree is this level of encouragement available today? And can we expect the Lord to fully invest Himself in our lives, despite our weakness and failure?

As the Bible demonstrates, God often reveals His greatness through human frailty. Regardless of who you are or what you have done, His divine grace is available to anyone willing to receive forgiveness and start over again. So take heart! The same God who inspired Jesus' followers to find hope in despair is the same God who lives in you. As with them, the failures you encounter in life are not impassable roadblocks, but momentary setbacks. Regardless of your performance, God is committed to your success and is eager to pick you up and place your feet back on the path of destiny.

Why does a holy God seem to overlook our many flaws and weakness when the Bible encourages us to be perfect?

While it's necessary to grow in godly character, we are yet in the process of maturing. Knowing this, Jesus, the man the book of Matthew portrays as the "Pearl of Great Price," sees our potential and loves us regardless of our imperfections. He knows that real pearls are recognized by their flaws, not their polished appearance. Like us, they are authentic, not because they are perfectly formed, but because their appearance reflects the blemishes produced by their harsh environment.

The lesson to ponder is that authentic pearls feel slightly rough to the touch, whereas flawless-looking pearls are usually fake. This concept is amply illustrated by Paul when he wrote in 2 Corinthians 12:10, "When I am weak, *then* am I strong." In the preceding verse, he clarifies this seeming contradiction, and boldly proclaims that God's strength is made perfect in our human weakness.

As most theologians will tell you, Paul's primary point in this passage of Scripture is indisputably clear. He was simply saying that our human imperfections are offset by the perfect grace of a perfect Creator. Undoubtedly we are flawed, but these imperfections only authenticate our existence as a fallen race in need of a Savior.

Things to Consider

Several brief statements are necessary to capture the theme of this chapter. First, your imperfections do not invalidate your potential to live an authentic existence, nor do your faults minimize the fulfillment of God's purpose for your life. Based on this reality, the greatest gift you can give yourself is the permission to fail and then try again. So never, never give up! With every breath you take there is yet hope for a better tomorrow.

> The greatest gift you can give yourself is the permission to fail.

Whatever your circumstance may be, always remember that it's a major accomplishment to wake up every morning to find you've survived the difficulties of yesterday. Regardless of your painful mistakes and blunders, you have made it this far. And if you continue to push forward and not give in to discouragement, success could one day knock on the door of your greatest failure. By merely recognizing the seed of success in your shortcomings, you maximize the opportunity to achieve your God-ordained purpose.

Also important to your journey is the ability to bring your whole being into alignment with your destiny. As you will see in the next chapter, the trick is to develop positive thoughts and words that will help cultivate your potential for success.

11

Creating Your Tomorrow

*"Deep within the soul of every believer is the light
of creativity that is released when they
declare by faith, 'Let there be!'"*

—Larry Randolph—

In addition to overcoming our limitations and mistakes, there are many other issues that greatly restrict our capacity to live an extraordinary life.

Visit any bookstore and you will find an extensive selection of books that are marketed with the promise of changing your life. The subject matter includes meditation, nutrition, exercise, astrology, positive thinking, and a host of other popular topics. In fact, my previous suggestions about how to deal with your personal constraints and failures have been thoroughly addressed by a myriad of writers throughout history.

After much reflection on this matter, therefore, I have decided to identify two things that have impacted my life the most— thought and speech. Both are innately connected to the evolution of human expression, beginning with thought and ending with language. Although each one bears the distinct mark of human intelligence, they are incomplete when separated from one another. Just as a river needs earthen banks to direct its flow, thoughts need language to convey their exact meaning.

Not surprisingly, these two dynamics have an enormous impact on our lives, drastically altering the world around us. Together they can set off a chain of events that will either launch us into our destiny or hinder our chances for success. When put into motion, the positive or negative "domino effect" of thought and speech has the power to sway the hearts of men, conquer nations, change cultures, and unfortunately create chaos. They are powerful activators that create our reality as well as our unreality.

What Are You Thinking?

It has been said that the human brain is the fragile dwelling place of the soul. If this is true, then our life experience begins with our thoughts and their impact on our state of being. Solomon summed it up nearly three thousand years ago when he wrote, "As a man thinks in his heart, so is he."

This long-standing reality is foundational to the practice of modern psychology. Most psychologists today believe that what we are (and all we become) is strongly influenced by a continuous stream of thoughts that run through our mind every day. This self-talk, as they call it, consists of positive and negative themes that create the reality in which we live. When our self-talk is negative, unfortunately, we develop irrational and harmful opinions of ourselves, which have a direct bearing on our attitude and behavior. When our self-talk is positive, on the other hand, we feel better about ourselves and are inclined to be more self-affirming and optimistic about life in general.

Besides its effect on the human psyche, our self-talk has a huge impact on our physical health. According to scientific research, the positive and negative aspects of our thought life strongly affect two chemicals that are released by the brain into our body. These two neurotransmitters (cortisol and serotonin) are vital to our well-being and play a significant role in the quality of our lives. High levels of either one can shorten or lengthen our time on Earth.

Scientists tell us, for example, that the chemical cortisol is a natural steroid hormone that is involved in a variety of bodily functions including the regulation of blood sugar, the immune system, and liver function. Recent findings show that a high cortisol level over an extended period of time can increase the risk of infection, high blood pressure, peptic ulcers, diabetes, osteoporosis, arterial fibrillation, and depression.

Serotonin, on the other hand, is the chemical that affects our mood and has a soothing effect on the nervous system. High levels of this natural "mood enhancer" are believed to boost endorphins and promote healing throughout the body. On the contrary, low levels of serotonin have been associated with medical conditions such as clinical depression, fibromyalgia, migraine headaches, irritable bowel syndrome, and various anxiety disorders.

The bottom line is that our self-talk is real and alive. With every thought, an electrical transmission goes across our brain releasing the two chemicals that I just mentioned. As stated, positive thoughts release high levels of serotonin that brings healing to our bodies, whereas negative thoughts release harmful levels of cortisol which is extremely detrimental to our health and well-being.

In simple terms, we are what we think. In fact, a number of experts believe that many of the diseases found in families are directly related to years of excessive negativity within the family line. Over several generations, these negative thoughts and words, which are passed from parent to child, can take a toll on the emotional and biological structure of an individual. The result is an assortment of mental and physical illnesses that are manifested in the family lineage. The outcome in many cases is premature death.

This could also be the reason for much of the financial and career failure that is repeatedly passed down from parent to child. It makes perfect sense, considering that it's extremely difficult to engage your destiny when you are battling poor health. In most instances, a deprived state of well-being will lower your quality of life and will greatly impede your drive for success.

Becoming What You Think

In spite of this problem, there is wonderful news. Studies show that it's possible to outsmart your negative brain patterns and reverse the curse of generational negativity in a relatively short period of time. The challenge is to develop positive self-talk that will purge your thought life of negative influences.

> To maximize your life, you must change your outlook from impossible to possible.

As I will address later on, you must stop believing lies about yourself and deal with the destructive thought patterns that limit your potential. Above all, you must change your outlook from impossible to possible and make sure your view of God and self is optimistic. In time, these things will become the tipping point for positive change in your life.

However, a word of caution is appropriate at this point. I'm not just talking about positive thinking that's an intellectual exercise separate from the Word of God. I'm talking about the act of thinking as God thinks. This means the Bible must be our point of reference for a positive lifestyle, promoting health and well-being. It's in this context that every promise in Scripture serves as a spiritual incubator that nurtures the hopes and dreams of mankind.

The underlying theme of this message comes across loud and clear in several Bible passages. For example, Joshua 1:8 declares that those who meditate on God's Word and obey His instructions will have abundant success. The New Testament also emphasizes the importance of this truth, instructing us in Philippians 4:8 to think on things that are pure, true, right, honorable, lovely, and good. Colossians 3:2 also advises us to set our heart and mind on uplifting things, not on things that bring us down.

In light of this reality, we must rethink what we have been thinking. Considering that the brain is hardwired for negativity by generations of destructive thought patterns, it's imperative that we reprogram our minds. The first step is to align our thinking with the disposition of Heaven portrayed in Scripture. The second step is learning to release creative power through our words as God did at the beginning of creation.

Words of Intent

If thoughts can influence the state of your well-being, then the verbalization of these thoughts have the power to alter the external world around you.

This means that intentional thoughts and words mixed with the force of faith can produce the same kind of creative power that spoke the universe into existence. As recorded in Genesis 1:3, the Creator declared His thoughts into the void of space and the cosmos sprang forth in a display of life—expanding in every direction virtually at the speed of light. The outcome, according to Hebrews 1:3, is that every thing in heaven and earth is now upheld by the power of that word.

Until recently, however, the creative potential of the spoken word has been recognized only by a few controversial Bible teachers and various members of the New Age movement. Fortunately, though, a new awareness of this phenomenon has emerged in the scientific and medical community through the groundbreaking study by researcher Dr. Masaru Emoto. In his controversial work about "speaking to water," Dr. Emoto provides unique insight into the power of words and the effect they have on our physical world—especially on water.

What put Dr. Emoto on the map is his claim that "words of intent" spoken over containers of water can actually change the expression of the water for good or bad. Dr. Emoto alleged that the molecular structure of water is affected by vibrations that come from words, music, and other forms of sound. The doctor's hypothesis, which he bases on the science of quantum physics, is that everything in the universe is pulsating on a molecular level. All forms of matter, including words and music, are individual collections of microscopic particles that vibrate at unique frequencies. As for water, it is a highly sensitive receptor that absorbs these external vibrations—drastically altering its natural state.

To prove this fascinating theory, Dr. Emoto developed a research technique using a powerful microscope and high-speed photography. In subzero temperatures, he photographed newly formed crystals of frozen water which were previously subjected to different kinds of words and music. He found that images of the ice crystals, which look like snowflakes under the microscope, were beautiful or ugly depending upon whether the words spoken over them were positive or negative.

For example, water that was exposed to negative language formed incomplete and irregular snowflake-like patterns with dull colors. In stark contrast, water that was exposed to kind and encouraging words displayed crystal patterns that were brilliant, complex, and colorful. The molecular transformation of the brilliant, healthy-looking crystals, claims Dr. Emoto, was achieved through prayer, soothing music, and positive words. Quite the opposite, the altered state of the dull and lifeless crystals was brought about by exposure to unkind words and loud, obnoxious music.

Creative Language

Given that the human body is composed of nearly seventy percent water, could this mean that we are seventy percent susceptible to the negative and positive influence of words?

Certainly, thoughts and words have energy and can be a friend or an enemy to your existence, altering the state of your environment. Still, it's a stretch to believe that positive words alone (especially those not mixed with faith in God) can instantly change the cellular structure of the human body. The more rational explanation is that the positive and negative chemicals released into our bodies by thoughts and words impact our emotional and mental disposition. And over time, they determine the condition of our physical health.

> What you think and say can either be a friend or an enemy to your existence.

On the other hand, Dr. Emoto's research may in theory give us a glimpse into the makeup of God's creative power. It's interesting to note in the Genesis 1 account of creation that God rearranged the molecular structure of space by simply declaring in verse three, "Let there be!" In a stunning display of power, He then commanded the waters below the heavens to be gathered into one place and called them seas. He called the dry land Earth and said, "It is good."

What does all this tell us? Can we also speak into existence our dreams and desires? Are we like God, as some believe, having the ability to create physical matter with the words of our mouth?

The answer is yes and no. Although we're not gods by any stretch of the imagination, Romans 5:17 implies that we are the children of God, being trained for rulership. As with a child of any sovereign, this rule begins by learning the power of a spoken command. In a shocking revelation about our authority as believers, Jesus said in Mark 11:23 that if our words were anchored in faith, we could say to a mountain, "Be removed and cast into the sea," and the mountain would obey us.

However, it's important to remember that our creative ability as humans is limited and will never equal the full creative status of God in this life. Certainly, I believe that the mountain-moving faith described by Jesus can change circumstances. I'm also aware that if you have absolute faith in God and believe what you say will happen, the forces that surround you will obey your command. But to create physical matter with our words or instantly change the cellular structure of the human body with verbal commands is a creative level very few people have attained.

Am I grateful for instantaneous healings and other creative miracles today?

Absolutely! But tragically, I know people who can produce the miraculous, but haven't developed positive self-talk that perpetuates their own well-being. Again, the spiritual principle of "process" comes into play. Although creative miracles are to be pursued and embraced, it's wise to start first with the power of positive words spoken over yourself.

It all begins and ends with the domino effect I talked about earlier. Your thoughts become words. Words create attitude.

Attitude determines your well-being. Well-being influences conduct. And over time, conduct will determine the shape of your destiny.

Although many in the New Age movement view this as a release of spiritual energy that's activated by positive words alone, I strongly disagree. As a Christian, I believe the creative force of faith is set in motion by language that is in sync with Scripture. I'm not referring to motivational thinking, mind-over-matter, or reaching a heightened state of consciousness through meditation. I'm talking about aligning your thoughts, speech, and attitude with the disposition of Heaven.

Basically, you have two choices. You can cast a spell on your life and curse yourself with negative words. Or you can speak to your "water" with positive self-talk that is anchored in biblical truth. Honestly, the more you talk and think like God, the more His Spirit is inclined to live big in your heart. Then again, the more negative you become, the more likely you are to invite dark forces to take up residence in your life. In either event, your thoughts and words can open or close your soul to the divine.

Reprogramming Your Life

When a computer is infected with a virus, the integrity of the hard drive is often compromised. The system and database become corrupted, and the programming is usually lost. In most cases, the only solution is to delete the corrupted files and reprogram the hard drive with new data.

The same is true of the harmful self-talk that makes its way into the hard drive of our brain. To deal with the problem, it's necessary to eliminate all negative thoughts and words and replace them with positive information. This "stop and start programming" (as I prefer to call it) works like a reset button for the human psyche.

The following list is designed to help rewire your thinking and assist you in the reprogramming process. To begin this process you must:

- Stop focusing on the negative circumstances in your life.
- Stop worrying about yesterday and tomorrow.
- Stop blaming yourself when something bad occurs.
- Stop anticipating the worst.
- Stop thinking that your life is a disaster.
- Stop saying that you are a failure.
- Stop stressing about your well-being.
- Stop dwelling on your shortcomings.
- Stop scrutinizing your performance.
- Stop believing your potential is limited.
- Stop sabotaging your potential with a negative attitude.
- Stop undermining your destiny with unbelief.

It's also crucial to make what I call "power declarations." These Bible-based declarations need to be verbalized over and over again with a sincere heart. For maximum results, you should:

- Start declaring, "I am a conqueror in life." (Romans 8:37)
- Start announcing, "I am strong in God." (Ephesians 3:16)
- Start claiming, "I am righteous through Christ." (2 Corinthians 5:21)
- Start professing, "I am loved by God." (1 John 4:19)

- Start pronouncing, "I am an heir of God."
  (Galatians 4:7)
- Start expressing, "I will overcome all negativity."
  (1 John 2:13)
- Start speaking, "I will lead a triumphant life."
  (2 Corinthians 2:14)
- Start confessing, "I will prosper and have success."
  (3 John 1:2)
- Start emphasizing, "I am more than capable."
  (1 John 4:4)
- Start speaking out, "I am created for greatness."
  (John 1:12)
- Start proclaiming, "I will fulfill my destiny."
  (Romans 8:28)
- Start saying, "I can do anything with God's help."
  (Philippians 4:13)

However, to fully complete the reprogramming process, you must carefully monitor the harmful nuances of your speech. You might consider exchanging negative words and phrases with positive ones. Try replacing:

- *Impossible* with ***possible***
- *Limited* with ***unlimited***
- *I can't* with ***I can***
- *I might* with ***I will***
- *What if* with ***why not***
- *No way* with ***always a way***
- *I'm not sure* with ***I'm certain***
- *Unattainable* with ***attainable***
- *Someday* with ***right now***

That's a lot to take in, so I want to encourage you to loosen up and give yourself a break. Try not to be uptight and overly serious. Take a deep breath and put a smile on your face. You might actually discover that life is easier when you learn to laugh and relax.

At the very least, you will find, like the researchers at the Loma Linda School of Medicine, that laughter is an excellent medicine. Their research shows in several studies that laughter decreases stress hormones and increases endorphins, which are the body's natural painkillers. In fact, the most significant changes in people who laughed regularly were found in the body's immune system. The positive effect was seen in the increase of a hormone that helps fight viruses and regulates healthy cell renewal.

Things to Consider

Considering the sum evidence of this chapter, it's important to change the way you think and talk. To live an extraordinary life, you must boldly step outside your limitations. You need to draw a line in the sand and say *no* to negativity and *yes* to a positive lifestyle.

To put it another way, you must live as though your future depends on your actions today. It's not always a quick fix and your world may not change overnight. Even so, the spiritual forces that God has designed to govern your life *will* be activated, setting in motion the creative power that will carry you to the threshold of your destiny. Once there, you will look back and see that you became what you were thinking and declaring yesterday.

PART
FOUR

Embracing the Fullness
of Your Destiny

12

Discovering Your Destiny

"There is no such thing as chance; and what seems to us merest accident springs from the deepest source of destiny."

—Johann Friedrich Von Schiller—
German poet and philosopher

"You and I have a rendezvous with destiny." This is the legendary line of a speech given by America's 40th president, Ronald Reagan. He went on to say that our actions greatly influence today's world as well as the hopes and dreams of future generations. The president summed up the subject in another quote by saying, "People should live their lives as a statement, not as an apology."

To what degree does this perspective affect the outcome of our lives? Are we truly responsible for the consequences of our actions? And if so, what level of accountability do we share in the unfolding of God's purpose for our life on Earth?

Many believe that mankind has very little responsibility for the fulfillment of their destiny. The only hope, according to some, is to live a moral and dutiful life that may one day lead to your purpose for being. They are convinced that destiny is not something you pursue; rather destiny is attracted to the person you become.

Although I respect the basic reasoning of this philosophy, I strongly believe there are specific things you can do to launch your destiny today. As mentioned in the previous chapter, thoughts and words are the architects of destiny and shape the very core of your existence. The process is simple, but powerful: Your thoughts become words, words produce actions, actions form habits, habits shape character, and character determines your tomorrow.

> You must plan for the future, because that's where you're going to spend the rest of your life.

Perhaps it was this reality that prompted Mark Twain to say, "You must plan for the future because that's where you are going to spend the rest of your life." Simply put, you can face tomorrow without purpose or you can make the decision to invest in the fulfillment of your destiny today. Either way, it's not chance but choice that determines your journey in life.

Destiny-Driven

The French novelist, Honoré de Balzac taught us that an unfilled destiny can drain the color from a person's entire existence. My interpretation of this quote is that our lives have very little meaning until destiny is discovered.

I believe this reality is true for each and every person on Earth. None of us will ever experience a bright future without awakening our passion to the fulfillment of our purpose. For this reason, we must cultivate hope for tomorrow and push through the restraints that keep us from reaching our full potential. The lesson here is that the pursuit of destiny is our insurance against a meaningless existence, while indifference destroys our sense of value and purpose.

This fundamental truth also applies to entire cultures and populations. In my travels around the world, I've noticed a common theme that runs throughout underprivileged nations. There appears to be a close connection between the depressed economies of a nation and the atmosphere of hopelessness and apathy that prevails among its citizens. It seems as though a lack of purpose attracts an unusual amount of despair, disease, and poverty, underscoring the message of Proverbs 29:18: "Where there is no vision, the people perish."

In contrast, societies that are purpose driven are more likely to contribute to the growth and progress of the human race. They seem to possess an inborn passion to improve their environment and are usually more advanced in the areas of science, medicine, and technology. In most cases, their *pursuit of purpose* is also the driving force behind the role they play as world leaders.

I know it's a bit of an overstatement to say that the self-worth of a population can be measured by its sense of purpose. But again, Proverbs implies that our well-being is determined by the value we place on our God-given destiny. In other words, we are limited not by our abilities but by our lack of vision.

That being the case, we must not give in to the apathy that exists in much of the world today—nor can we afford to nurture a survival mentality, drifting aimlessly from one day to another. Like many great men and women throughout history, our challenge is to overcome the many obstacles in our path that threaten our God-given right to lead a purposeful life.

Divine Purpose

Each one of us must believe that we are here at this exact time in history for a reason that's far greater than living out the ordinary routine of everyday life. Jesus of Nazareth provided a classic example of this truth when He defended His own destiny to Pontius Pilate, the Roman governor of Judea. When asked about His reason for being on Earth, the Lord simply replied in John 18:37, "For this I have been born, and for this I have come into the world, to testify to the truth."

It's interesting to note that Jesus' defense was not based solely on His right to exist, but on the *purpose* of His existence. He boldly wielded the authority to impact His generation on the premise that His life was the product of destiny, not chance. He understood, as William Barclay put it nearly two thousand years later, that "There are two great days in a person's life: the day we are born and the day we discover why."

What lessons can we learn from the Lord's pursuit of His purpose in life? Are we expected to live our lives today with the same conviction of heart?

This timeless illustration shows us the far-reaching impact of a life lived under the influence of divine purpose. We can also see that *purpose* is life's great motivator, setting in motion our potential for greatness. Apparently, our Lord understood this truth and demonstrated to mankind the divine motivation for the air we breathe. He knew that the purpose of life is to live a life of purpose.

With this in mind, my hope is that our generation will one day reach a place of discovery that will define our reason for being. I'm also hopeful that our individual destinies will, in a collective sense, shape the course of history for the better. Anything less than a purpose-driven life is an indictment against the example set by Jesus and brings to light the words of the nineteenth-century poet Edward Bulwer-Lytton:

"We are but as the instrument of Heaven. Our work is not design, but destiny."

Talent and Gifting

If you don't find your destiny, life will impose one upon you. The choice is yours to make. Either you will embrace your God-inspired purpose or relinquish it to fate. In the end, you alone are accountable to God for what you do with such a treasured endowment as destiny.

Based on this truth, every one of us must accept the challenge to discover God's unique design for our lives. However, the difficulty lies in the often-indistinguishable difference between a person's talent, gifting, occupation, and destiny. For example, some people have a destiny that's shaped solely by the strength of their gifting. They seem to possess gifts and talents that are complementary to their life-purpose and make little or no distinction between their gifting today and the role it plays in their future destiny.

For others, however, the opposite seems to be true. In spite of being highly gifted, they never seem to touch the reality of their purpose in life. Although impressive, their gifts and talents don't necessarily ensure the fulfillment of their destiny. Regrettably, some of the most gifted people I know seem lost in this world, hopelessly adrift in a sea of uncertainty.

On a personal level, I have watched this scenario played out on both sides of my family line. Several of my relatives, though poorly educated, were greatly endowed with natural talents and spiritual gifts. My grandfather, for example, possessed an extraordinary musical talent and a knack for poetry. My mother shared his musical ability and was also a skilled sketch artist. Dad was more spiritually inclined and excelled in the gifts of divine healing and prophecy.

The tragedy, though, was that most of my family somehow failed to cultivate their purpose for being. This was especially true of my beloved father. Although highly gifted, he wasn't able to maximize his life-purpose and seemed to suffocate from feelings of hopelessness and despair. Other than an occasional encounter with the outside world, the impact of his gifting was limited to our family and a handful of people in our little church. Sadly, this godly man who possessed so much raw potential passed away without fully understanding why he was here on Earth.

I, too, have faced the same challenge in life. As a young man, I was naturally gifted as an artist and musician. Between the two, music was my greater passion and absorbed every moment of my life. For many years, I worked hard at becoming a professional musician. Then one day, something in my heart changed and I knew that God had another plan for my future. He made it clear that my destiny lay elsewhere—in the area of spiritual ministry.

Was a change of such magnitude easy?

Of course not! But I was determined to find my place in life no matter how long it took. From that point forward, I began to pursue my primary calling and put my passion for music on the back burner.

Gift Shift?

Was I wrong to pursue my musical talent as a young man? Did I waste my time cultivating something that was not my main purpose in life?

As I've already indicated, all talent should be appreciated and nourished—and on many occasions a person's talent is complementary to their life calling. For others, however, their natural talent is often secondary to what they are destined to become. Many times, the gifting that takes center stage in their early years is not necessarily their primary purpose in life, but rather a bridge to their ultimate destiny.

For example, the gift of dream interpretation that resided in the Bible character Joseph served him well as a young man and played a major role in his ascent to the throne of Egypt. As depicted in Genesis 41, this particular endowment brought him recognition and eventually led the soon-to-be ruler to his life-purpose. After reaching his ultimate destiny, however, the Bible never makes reference to this gift again. Once he was there, other gifts and talents came into play—such as the gifts of administration and leadership.

Clearly, Joseph's ability to adapt to different seasons of life was the secret of his success. And just as this young man modified his gifting to accommodate a shift of purpose, you and I should consider the wisdom of being flexible.

> The secret of success lies in your ability to adapt to different seasons of life.

All I'm saying is: Don't limit your potential for growth and change. Like Joseph, you must make room for the unknown factors in life and never lock yourself into a narrow mindset about the scope of your destiny. Of course, you should be thankful for your natural abilities, but make sure they're not counterproductive to your future purpose in life.

It might be helpful, therefore, to ask yourself the following questions: Is this the season to develop the more obvious talents and gifts in my life? Or is it time to step out into an undefined purpose and activate other gifting that may be more compatible with my ultimate destiny?

Because the situation differs from person to person, only you and God can determine what stage of life you are presently living in. Whatever your circumstance, though, keep in mind that the cycle of life is made up of many seasons. Again, that means your heart should be open to change. You must realize that flexibility is not a negative quality, but rather a blessing. After all, the ability to adapt may be one of the greatest survival tools you will ever possess.

Vocation or Destiny?

None of us are exempt from the challenge to become what we were created to be. As I have suggested, those who are abundantly gifted must evaluate whether or not their natural talent is in harmony with their God-given destiny. At some point in time, it might be necessary to decide whether to maintain your present course or embrace the possibility of a life-altering change.

The same option applies to a person's occupation. Especially at risk are people who command successful careers but feel as though they haven't discovered their true purpose for being. Whether by choice or chance, they often surrender themselves to a career that is out of step with God's master plan for their lives. Over time, their inner struggle becomes so unbearable that they fall into a painful season of deep soul-searching.

If this is your life story, be encouraged. You are not alone in the process. Many people throughout the Bible had vocations that had to be put into proper perspective. For example, Elisha was a farmer prior to his calling, and both Amos and Moses were sheepherders before discovering their calling as prophets. The beloved King David began his life as a musician and songwriter, and the prophet Daniel first served as governor of Babylon. Remarkably, the Son of God began His own journey on Earth as a carpenter (1 Kings 19:16; Amos 1; Exodus 3:1; 1 Samuel 16:16; Daniel 2:48; Mark 6:3).

This common scenario is also seen in the lives of great men and women over the last several hundred years. The legendary Vincent Van Gogh, for example, served as a missionary to Belgium before discovering his calling as an artist. Wilbur and

Orville Wright, the innovators of flight, managed a printing firm and bicycle shop as young men. Benjamin Franklin was an accomplished musician and composer before finding his role in politics. The renowned aviator Amelia Earhart, who received many prestigious awards for being the first woman to fly solo nonstop across the Atlantic, began her life working as a nurse and enrolled in college to study medicine. Then there's the famous astronomer Edward Hubble, who began his career as a basketball coach but was later awarded the "Catherine Wolfe Bruce Gold Medal" for discoveries that forever changed the way mankind views the universe.

However, the opposite scenario is also true. There are other men and women throughout history who had occupations directly related to their life's purpose. The list includes William Shakespeare, Wolfgang Mozart, Abraham Lincoln, Albert Einstein, Florence Nightingale, and a host of other people who possessed a specific gift from their youth that was consistent with their destiny as adults. Their purpose in life seemed to flow naturally from their talent and there was little distinction between their gifting, occupation, and reason for being.

There are also countless examples seen in modern society. Whether a housewife, brain surgeon, or musician, many people today are fulfilling a God-ordained destiny that was bestowed upon them at conception. And for the most part, they are well-adjusted members of society who are content with their divine mission in life. Because their contribution to society is one and the same with their destiny, they play an invaluable role in the fulfillment of God's plan for their generation.

How do we know if our vocation is actually synchronized with our destiny?

To be honest, the answer can be challenging and requires careful consideration. However, one of the first signs that a person's life is out of balance with their divine purpose is an overwhelming sense of unhappiness. Deep inside their soul is a nagging feeling that life has somehow passed them by. No matter how hard they work or how great their successes, they feel empty—their heart heavy with regret and disappointment.

On the other hand, a good indicator that a person's career and destiny are in harmony is a sense of peace in their soul. Because their vocation *is* their reason for being, they feel no need to launch a search for purpose. Deep inside is an assurance that their life's work is more than a career, it's their divine calling. They are more than happy to do what they do and often exude a sense of fulfilled purpose. In many ways, their lives exemplify a quote by Vincent Van Gogh:

> "Your destiny is not your profession that brings home your paycheck. Your destiny is what you were put on Earth to do and become—with such passion and intensity that it becomes spiritual in calling."

Destiny-in-Waiting

Regardless of where you are in the process of life, there is hope for the fulfillment of your destiny. The good news is that God created you for a unique purpose and has allotted enough time for you to accomplish that purpose. This means you have ample opportunity to fulfill your calling, regardless of how many times you have failed or how many times you have traveled down the wrong path in life. No matter what your circumstances are, there is always time to become what you were created to be.

Both secular and biblical history shows us that you're never too old or too young to engage your life-purpose. For example, David was a young boy when he killed Goliath the Philistine giant and freed Israel from oppression. Joseph ascended to the throne of Egypt at thirty-three years of age, and Jesus was thirty when He began His earthly ministry. The musical genius Mozart wrote his first composition at five years old, and Thomas Edison invented the light bulb at the age of thirty-two.

In contrast, other distinguished men in history were well advanced in age before reaching their calling in life. Moses was eighty years old when he was commissioned to deliver the people of God from slavery, and his successor, Joshua, was seventy when he took command of the nation of Israel. George Washington was fifty-seven years old when he was elected president, and Benjamin Franklin was seventy-nine when he became the governor of Pennsylvania. The genius Einstein was named "Person of the Century" by *Time Magazine* forty-four years *after* he died.

Considering these wide-ranging examples, several factors come into play.

First, whether you are young or old, unfulfilled destiny may be your best defense against premature death. If you are actively engaged in the pursuit of your life-purpose, nothing and no one but God can send you to the next life before your time. No matter how long it takes, destiny will wait for those who harbor great expectations for their future and take the necessary steps to get there. As the Roman philosopher Lucius Annaeus Senecathe once said, "Destiny leads the willing and patiently awaits the reluctant."

Also, bear in mind that destiny is faithful to take you where you need to go—not necessarily where you want to go. So don't fight the process and stop worrying about your future. You're called to live a life of purpose, not a life of fear and anxiety. According to Winston Churchill:

> "It is a mistake to try to look too far ahead. The chain of destiny can only be grasped one link at a time."

Things to Consider

As we have seen, many people have an occupation that's in harmony with their destiny. For others, their occupation is what they do—their destiny is what they become.

If you fit the last category and feel as though you're living a life that's inconsistent with your God-breathed destiny, I have some encouragement to offer. First, don't give up! Have faith in the providence of God and refuse to give in to despair. Be hopeful and believe in the promise of Psalm 138:8 that God is at work perfecting everything that concerns your life.

Most of all, remember that no one but you can give to your generation the unique God-deposit that you alone possess. And because you have a special place to fill in this world, never settle for second best or an imitation of your destiny. In every way, the expression of your purpose must be real and authentic, clearly setting you apart from all others.

What's more, it will take the fulfillment of your distinct role in life to reveal the harmony that God wants to bring to this planet. The most important question is: Will you hide from your unique contribution to society? Or are you willing to express your individuality for the sake of true unity?

CHAPTER

13

Harmonizing Your Destiny

"If we are to achieve a richer culture, richer in contrasting values, we must recognize the whole gamut of human potentialities... one in which each diverse human gift will find a fitting place."

—Margaret Mead—
American anthropologist and author

Since the dawning of creation, there has been a dance of opposites present in the universe. As illustrated in the book of Genesis, God created a vast assortment of polar opposites and brought them together in a symphony of diversity that defies description.

In brilliant fashion, the Creator synchronized the darkness of night with the light of day, the chill of winter with the warmth of summer, mountains with valleys, deserts with oceans—on and on goes the endless list of opposites bound together in a harmonious display of intelligent design. Without this dance of opposites, the universe as we know it today would simply not exist. And even if it were able to survive in some homogeneous form, it would still be boringly sterile.

As I talked about in chapter one, the Creator's design for the universe is extremely fascinating and is not limited to the formation of the elements. In fact, one of the most amazing aspects of God's creativity has to do with the unique role that each person is destined to play in the unification of His overall purpose for Earth. Like the diverse workings of the cosmos, each member of the human race is destined to contribute their gifts and talents to the whole of society without compromising the integrity of their individuality. This contribution is perhaps one of the most important assignments given to humanity.

To accomplish this task, there are several obstacles that must be addressed. One major hindrance is the often misunderstood distinction that's related to the concept of unity and uniformity. Also problematic is the tension that exists between the notion of "harmonized diversity" and the ideology of "sameness." In my opinion, these issues have created more problems for the progress of society and religion than any other issues today.

Unity or Uniformity?

In order to deal with the difficulties mentioned above, we must first focus on the stark contrast between unity and uniformity. Understanding their distinction is not just a matter of correctness, but is extremely important to how people fit into the spiritual and social environment in the real world. Because of the great disparity between these two concepts (and the way they affect our capacity to coexist as a community on Earth), the following definitions are necessary.

First, uniformity is often described in many dictionaries as an "unvarying conformity to a pattern or rule that results in a sense of overall sameness." It's a standardization of action and thought that lacks diversity to the point of boredom. Artistically, it refers to an appearance of sameness that has no variance in texture, color, or design. In a religious context, uniformity is total conformity to one standard or rule of religious expression without regard to individual creativity.

Unity, on the other hand, has a fundamentally opposite meaning. It is by definition the quality of being united in spirit and purpose without the loss of individual expression. From an artistic viewpoint, it's the harmony among individual elements of a work of art or piece of literature that results in a total unified expression. The same is true of unity in religion. It, too, can be characterized as a totality of diverse parts joined in harmony of spirit and purpose, while honoring the right of individual thought and expression at the same time.

Practically speaking, one of the best examples to highlight the difference between unity and uniformity is found in the world of music. Experts tell us that the beauty of music lies in its diverse originality, not in its uniformity. This is undeniably true of the musical tension found in an orchestra or other performing groups. Clearly, it's the dance of opposing sounds and tones among a variety of instruments that creates a beautiful symphony. The challenge is for each instrument to maintain the integrity of its distinct sound, while at the same time harmonizing with the whole group.

> The beauty of true unity is found in diversity and originality, not in uniformity.

The same principle also applies to other areas of life—the most common being the unity found in a healthy business or corporation. No successful firm would want its employees to act and think exactly the same. Of course, there are uniform standards and protocol set by the establishment that must be respected. But like it is with an orchestra, the hallmark of a thriving, successful company is the unity created by the different contributions of each person—

not an irrational commitment to uniformity. It is simply the collective differences (submitted to the whole) that makes an organization work as a productive unit.

The Sameness Fallacy

As you can see, unity through diversity is perhaps one of the highest forms of intelligence seen in modern society. In fact, it is our God-inspired capacity to think independently together that gives us a freedom of expression that is priceless. Regarding this subject, the notable Chief Justice of the Supreme Court Charles Evans Hughes, wrote:

> "When we lose the right to be different, we lose the privilege to be free."

This quote has special meaning for people of faith today. In modern society there's an ever-increasing polarization between the notion of diversified unity and that of uniformity. Because of this controversy, many believers are deeply divided over the ideology of "sameness" versus "individual expression."

Those who hold to the sameness mentality, for example, believe that true unity is attained through doctrinal harmony alone. They are convinced that everyone must see "eye to eye" in their interpretation of Scripture, and often spend their lives advocating uniformity under the banner of unity.

Quite the opposite, others who embrace "individualism" see the "sameness mindset" as being deceptive. They are reluctant to comply and often shrink back from anything that undermines their right to live a unique, spiritual life. There are determined to protect their uniqueness, even at the cost of social isolation.

Who is right? Is unity through diversity a more biblical model than uniformity? And if so, what threat does the practice of uniformity pose for the advancement of society and religion in today's world?

Whatever your views may be, keep in mind that history demonstrates that our best efforts to achieve sameness are less than favorable. For centuries, in fact, misguided people and their organizations have struggled to standardize every aspect of human expression. In an attempt to create a humanistic form of unity, they have neutralized diverse spectrums of human uniqueness and independence. Their goal is to stifle all creative expressions of individuality, redirecting every unique reflection of mankind back through their prism of uniform thinking.

The problem with this mentality is that the suppression of individual expression stands in direct opposition to God's purpose for diversity. From the unified effort to build the Tower of Babel to ancient Rome's attempt to unite its citizens into one ideological and religious mindset, the outcome has been disastrous. In the same manner, the dogma of socialism in the twentieth century was so limiting to the individuality of its citizens that productivity in communist countries declined at an alarming rate.

Historically, any attempt to achieve unity through uniformity on a secular or religious scale has been a complete failure. Not surprisingly, the Bible predicts the same scenario will resurface in the "last days," warning us that every person and religion will be at risk from a toxic form of pseudo-unity that's lethal to true spiritual harmony. As seen in Revelation 13, this ideology of sameness will mutate into a global movement, promoting uniformity under the umbrella of unity. The awful truth is that people refusing to bear the mark of uniformity will be alienated from mainstream society.

The Beauty of Opposites

What can we do to protect our God-given uniqueness? How does modern society avoid an age-old deception that wants to absorb our individual lives into an ideology of conformity?

Where there is no difference, all that remains is indifference. Unless we make room for unique expressions of individuality, we are doomed to a colorless existence that has little regard for variety or authenticity. The outcome is a dull, lifeless world that is creatively void and steeped in apathy.

On a small scale, I have battled this issue throughout the course of my own life and ministry. As a pastor, I've had to make a difficult decision between bringing people on staff that share my views and strengths or hire those who excel in the area of my weakness. The same is true of my traveling ministry today. Because I'm aware that it takes the positive and negative charge of a battery to produce energy, I am committed to the principle of harmonized diversity. As a result, I often minister with people who are different in style, thought, and experience.

Although the process can be challenging, I have discovered the immense value of diversity. One good example occurred in the 1980s after I moved my ministry base from Arkansas to Southern California. At the onset, I had a choice to travel with believers who had ministries similar to my own or do something totally out of the box. I eventually chose the latter, and for a season I traveled with a contemporary Christian rap and dance group.

The protest from several of my peers was intense. They just couldn't see the value of a young, ethnically diverse Christian rap group from Los Angeles leading worship for a middle-aged white man from the South. To tell the truth, I was not sure it would work either. All I knew is that I had something they needed, and they had something I needed. In the exchange, my heart was stirred by a generation desperate for the Father's love, and they in turn found guidance and encouragement from me.

Several years later, when I became the pastor of a church in the Orange County area, I followed the same convictions about diversity and staffed my church with people unlike myself. Again the protest was loud when I chose men and women who were polar opposites in personality and gifting. Naturally, the challenges that came with such an assorted group of leaders were not easy to handle. But in spite of the difficulties, the church seemed to benefit from a diversity of leadership, which I believed was more biblical than the sameness model adopted by many of my peers. Thankfully, the congregation was given the opportunity to see a wide-ranging expression of God's gifts and talents that I alone could not provide.

I'm aware that this principle is not suitable for every leadership team, and it may be unrealistic for leaders with a busy schedule to find the time to deal with a diversity of voices and gifting. But for me, the best model for spiritual leadership is found in the diversity of gifts and talents that bring harmony to God's purpose for mankind. I have found that healthy ministry is achieved by placing our weaknesses and strengths side by side and permitting them to speak to one another—not by sacrificing our individuality for a fake form of unity.

Unity in Tension

Although diversity may be the most difficult thing for the Western Church to embrace, it's perhaps the most dangerous thing to ignore. Any attempt to suppress the uniqueness of a person or people group for the sake of uniformity must be labeled for what it is: a *false* gospel of unity.

To set the record straight, we must demonstrate to the world that true unity is oneness of spirit, not sameness of thought and expression. We must defend the right of every person of faith to be themselves, regardless of their intellectual, emotional, and spiritual color.

Am I saying that believers should live as nonconformists, flaunting their individuality in the face of others?

The answer is a resounding no. By no means should we lead independent lives without regard for the collective purpose of God on Earth. Nor can we disregard the biblical mandate for true unity and create discord among those He has called us to work with side by side. Actually, it would be foolish to believe there are no biblical standards or collective purposes for people of faith to rally around.

Then again, it's also unwise to engage in religious activity without embracing the concept of harmonized diversity. As I mentioned earlier, we have only to look at the diverse workings of the universe to see the genius of this principle. Just as the gears and wheels of a mechanical clock move in opposite directions to keep perfect time, the diverse elements of the universe are synchronized in such a way as to produce "unity in tension."

> True unity creates a symphony of movement that can be achieved only by the collective contribution of diverse individuals and their unique gifting.

Again, my point is that true unity creates a symphony of movement that can only be achieved by the collective contribution of diverse individuals and their unique gifting. In 1 Corinthians chapter 12, Paul recognizes this tension as being descriptive of the life and nature of the universal Church and explains how the diversity of each individual member of Christ's Church serves as a catalyst for the unification of the whole body. He makes it clear that without the tension of unity, our function as a body of believers would be awkward and uncoordinated— much like a toddler trying to walk for the first time.

What more can I say except that being true to yourself and discovering your individual destiny is not an option, but a necessity. In the same way that the muscles of the human body work in total opposition to each other to ensure proper balance and harmony, all the members of God's family must work together to create a concert of spiritual harmony. The challenge is to express your own individuality without being in discord with others.

Honestly, it all comes down to a few important thoughts. As I've stated abundantly throughout this book, the true art of living is learning to appreciate the value of your individuality and exercising your right to be different. Then again, the fact that you're different in personality, thought, and theology doesn't mean you should have a disagreeable attitude. After all, your individuality should be expressed as a loving, positive contribution, not as a hindrance to others.

Different Strokes

Throughout the last two millennia, the mindset of sameness has challenged the spirit of creativity in the global Church. In my own lifetime, I have witnessed several movements bottom out in the mud of religious conformity. Some eventually recovered and moved forward, and others refused to embrace diversity and remained inside the box of traditional thinking.

During the 1960s and '70s, for example, many in the Church began to cry out for fresh encounters with God. Much to their surprise, the answer came in the form of a young generation of hippies who were unorthodox in attitude and lifestyle. As a result, believers with a mindset of religious uniformity were deeply offended. They couldn't imagine true spirituality being birthed through such radical, free-spirited youth and came to oppose a young generation that was suffocating from the stale air of dead religion.

Tragically, thousands of these young seekers were shunned by traditional believers of their day. Because of their long hair, bohemian fashion, and edgy musical taste, they were not considered "church-friendly." As a result, many were forced to leave mainstream denominations to search for spirituality elsewhere. Some found refuge in less conservative churches, while others came together to worship in home groups and other small gatherings.

Ironically, their rejection by religious conservatives became a launching pad for a remarkable youth revival that was later known as the Jesus Movement. Out of this movement came the birth of contemporary gospel music that produced songs about unity, change, and spiritual freedom. Meanwhile, the traditional church dug their heels in and fiercely clung to old choruses about exclusion and separation from worldly people.

Thank God, over the last few decades, diversity of fashion and musical style has become more acceptable in the religious world. You can visit most churches in America today and find a cross section of people who look, act, and think differently. Everything from high fashion to jeans and T-shirts can be seen in congregations that are culturally diverse reflections of our postmodern world.

Where will this path ultimately lead us? I'm not exactly sure, but such diversity is wonderfully refreshing and is largely due to the change brought about by discontented youth who refused to conform just for the sake of conformity. They taught us that God is more concerned about reaching the heart of a generation than He is with their appearance and musical taste. The unmistakable message is that God loves diversity and is delighted when people are secure enough to embrace their individuality.

For this reason alone, we must not devalue our differences, nor minimize the unique role each person plays in God's family. Just as a diversity of animals converged on Noah's Ark in biblical times, a diverse spectrum of humanity will soon be given an opportunity to unite in a marvelous and colorful exhibition of God's glory in the earth. In the end, the kingdoms of this world will feel the impact of God's eternal purpose to unite all things into the ultimate purpose of Christ.

Things to Consider

Among the lessons to be learned in this chapter, harmony through diversity is perhaps the most important. Without the delicate balance of unity in tension, religious institutions often mutate into a mindset of sameness and suffer a mediocre existence. Sadly, this unhealthy evolution reflects less and less of the Creator's enormous diversity and more of an outward appearance of uniformity.

I'm not saying that every person or church must be different for the sake of being different. Nor am I suggesting that every expression of a person's spirituality is a unique reflection of God's personality. I'm simply saying that there is room for diversity of gifting in this world. In fact, your individual contribution should be as unique as a single stroke of color on a painter's canvas, while at the same time complementing the overall beauty of the picture.

The challenge is learning to express your individuality without becoming dogmatic—insisting on your own way. You are free to be different, but you should avoid a disagreeable attitude at any cost. For your diversity to be healthy, your individual contribution should be like the missing piece of a puzzle that brings completion to the whole picture. Even though you're a unique individual, you must work with others for the common good, being united in heart and purpose.

Equally important to your life's journey are the appointed moments in time that open you up to radical encounters with the supernatural realm. As you will see in the final chapter, these spiritual gateways lead to a place reserved for those who dare to pursue their ultimate destiny. And if you're willing to make this journey without regard to cost or convenience, you will eventually find yourself standing at destiny's door. In the words of the renowned British poet Robert Browning, "The best is yet to be."

14

The Ultimate Quest

*"Man's ultimate destiny is to become one with the
Divine Power which governs and sustains
the creation and its creatures."*

—Alfred A. Montaper—
American author

Throughout this book, I've talked extensively about God's creative genius and His diversity in humanity. I explained the significance of valuing ourselves as authentic human beings, discovering our unique gifting, breaking through our personal constraints, and maximizing our failures. I also addressed the benefits of living a positive life, and I discussed the distinct role that our individual destinies play in the shaping of God's purpose on Earth.

At this point, though, I must confess that these topics are intended to lead you to a fundamental but profound truth. The urgent message is: Prepare for the habitation of a loving God who wants to live big in your life. I know it sounds too good to be true, but Revelation 3:20 portrays Jesus persistently knocking on the door of our heart, saying, "If anyone hears My voice and opens the door, I will come in to him and will dine with him, and he with Me."

In a similar way, Song of Solomon captures this appeal for intimacy in symbolic language that speaks of Christ and His church. In a riveting scene in chapter five, the author describes the shepherd lingering at the cottage door of the Shulamite bride, pleading, "Open to me, my sister, my darling, my dove, my perfect one! For my head is drenched with dew, my locks with the damp of night." Moved with passion for his bride, the shepherd thrusts his hand through the opening in the door, desperately seeking to unlatch the lock that separates them.

God's Dwelling Place

Why such dramatic symbolism? Why the assumption that the Great Shepherd wants to make His home in the heart of something as frail as human flesh? Was Solomon suggesting that the Creator is searching for a way to reveal His glory through mankind?

In earlier writings in the Old Testament, Solomon spoke eloquently about this subject. In his prayer of dedication in 2 Chronicles 6:14-41, he established two distinct themes, saying:

> "Oh Lord, the God of Israel, there is no god like You in Heaven." Solomon then made a declaration that seemed somewhat out of sync with the first statement: "Behold, Heaven and the highest heaven cannot contain You.... Now therefore arise, O Lord God [and come down] to Your resting place."

Considering the precise language used in this prayer, it's apparent that Solomon understood the complexity of this paradoxal truth. He clearly recognized the Creator's majesty in the heavens, but he was also aware of the impossibility of God's majesty being entirely revealed through the cosmos alone. Undoubtedly, it was on this premise that he implored the Almighty to come down and dwell in His resting place, which, of course, was the people of Israel and the temple they had built for Him.

What is even more amazing is Solomon's assumption that God would want to actually live among men. As mentioned earlier, this inspired writer seemed to grasp the long-standing intention of the Creator's heart for intimacy, and he wove that longing into the storyline of the Song of Solomon. The central theme of this beautiful work, although metaphorical, was that God desired to express His glory through mankind and would go to extreme measures to invest Himself in the heart and soul of humanity.

From Garden to Temple

When and where was this passion for intimacy awakened in the heart of God?

Without a doubt, the divine quest of the Creator began long before the lifetime of Solomon. The book of Genesis reveals that God was on a journey, searching for various ways and means to express His fullness on Earth. As outrageous as it may seem, the omnipotent Creator, who has no need to show off His glory or prove Himself to anyone, appeared to be searching for a place to make His abode—even if He had to create one.

This reality is clearly seen in the creation of Adam and Eve in the Garden of Eden. In a remarkable way, the novel event portrayed in the Genesis account brings to light God's plan to set up housekeeping on Earth and showcase His glory through the human race. Genesis 3 tells us, in fact, that the Creator visited Adam and Eve, the crowning glory of His creation, and communed with them on a daily basis. Not only were these two created beings the object of God's affection, they had, in a sense, become His earthly dwelling place.

Regrettably, Adam and Eve fell from grace and were forced to leave their beautiful paradise. As recorded in Genesis 3:24, an angel with a flaming sword sealed off the entrance to the Garden of Eden, closing the doors on a piece of history that could only be redeemed in another dispensation of time. The irony was beyond imagination. Sadly, the Almighty was now without a human friend on Earth— alone in a paradise created for intimacy between the Creator and His creation.

> When Adam and Eve were removed from Eden, God was without a human friend— alone in a paradise created for intimacy with His beloved creation.

With the passing of generations, however, something incredible began to unfold. As you may remember from chapter two, the adventure that began in the Garden of Eden in the first few pages of Genesis spilled over into the book of Exodus.

In meticulous detail, Exodus 25-27 reveals God's transition from a garden environment to a wilderness tabernacle, built under the supervision of Moses. Although completely inanimate, this tabernacle was a reflection of the Creator's collective glory—a place where He could dwell among the descendents of Adam and Eve.

For a while, God seemed to be at home in this environment, living in a secret world behind a veil in the "innermost court" of the desert sanctuary. But aside from the charm and beauty of the Old Testament tabernacle, there remained in His heart a desire to connect with mankind on a more personal level. Although adequate for the moment, His new home was not His preferred habitation. As recorded in Exodus 20:19, it was merely a concession for a people who were fearful to engage the Almighty "face to face. "

God's Forwarding Address

A quick look at the writings of the Old Testament prophets tells us that God had become disenchanted with the pretense of ritual and ceremony. The Creator seemed to be weary of animal sacrifices and yearned to move out of an impersonal temple of wood and stone into houses of flesh and blood. In terms of a personal relationship, He longed to share Himself once again with human beings who could appreciate the affection of His heart.

Such an assumption is logical when you consider the strong language used in Isaiah 1:11-14:

> "I'm sick of your burnt offerings of rams and the fat of fattened cattle...When you come to worship Me, who asked you to parade through My courts with all your ceremony? Stop bringing Me your meaningless gifts; the incense of your offerings disgusts Me! As for your celebrations of the New Moon and the Sabbath and your special days for fasting—they are all sinful and false. I want no more of your pious meetings."

Also, other Bible passages resonate this cry of God's heart by predicting a coming change of protocol. In 1 Chronicles 16:24, David stated that the Almighty would show His glory to the Gentiles and His marvelous works among the nations. And as mentioned earlier in this chapter, his son Solomon echoed this same desire in his writings. Likewise, Isaiah 66:18 revealed God's ultimate intention and declared that His majesty would someday be revealed through mankind and all flesh would experience His glory.

All of this, of course, was speaking of God's future resting place in the coming Messiah, the New Testament Church, and beyond. Yet how and when was this going to happen? How long would it take the Creator to relocate from an Old Testament address to a more permanent residence in the New Testament? Would God be homeless once again? Would He be caught in transition until the Messianic prophecy of Isaiah 7:14 was finally fulfilled?

Though many centuries would come and go, the scenario was finally played out as Isaiah had predicted. Luke 1:35 tells us that the Spirit of God overshadowed a young virgin named Mary who surrendered herself to the Immaculate Conception of a God-child. Although this God-child was known by His contemporaries as Jesus of Nazareth, His Old Testament name was Immanuel, meaning "God with us." In either case, He was as the Gospels portrayed—the brightness of God's glory and the exact image of His person.

Perhaps this was in Paul's mind when he suggested in 1 Corinthians 15:45 that Jesus was the "second Adam" who embodied the light of God's radiant glory. The bottom line is that the Creator had clothed Himself in human flesh and was dwelling once again among the sons of Adam and Eve.

Home at Last

Now for the more obscure part of the journey:

When God (in human form) grew up to walk among men, a religious leader asked Him about His dwelling place. Jesus unexpectedly replied in Matthew 8:20, "Foxes have holes and the birds have nests, but the Son of Man has nowhere to lay His head." Then in a statement that seemed completely out of context with the question, He said in verse 22, "Follow Me."

What did the Lord mean? Wasn't God's ultimate dwelling place now in Christ, and wasn't the eternal abode of Christ now in God, as written in John 10:38? And what about the "Follow Me" statement? Was Jesus calling us to a physical location on

Earth, or was He talking about something greater—about a mysterious and yet undisclosed place known only to prophets and angels?

No doubt, most of Jesus' disciples understood that the Creator had moved from Eden and numerous temples to take up residence in the God-man they were following. Yet in reality, the transition was incomplete—having much broader implications than anyone could ever imagine. There was, as the prophets of old had indicated, the unfolding of an age-old mystery in which God would fill all creation with Himself. The irony was that God, now present in the "second Adam," was still not totally at home on Earth. He was not completely at rest until such time that He could lay down His head in the "second Eve"—a collective body of believers.

How and where was this going to take place? And by what means would the Almighty and recreate the Garden of Eden on a spiritual level?

As predicted throughout the Old Testament, it would take the ultimate sacrifice of God's Son on a wooden altar for the plan to come together. As unbelievable as it may seem, Christ's sacrificial death for the sins of humanity brought an end to the curse of separation from God and the beginning of new life for all mankind. There was at last a chance to receive forgiveness and reconnect with the Creator.

In a sweeping exposé in 1 Corinthians 15, Paul put this truth into proper perspective. He surmised that all humanity had lost their home because of Adam's transgression—but through the sacrifice of the "second Adam," we have been given a rare opportunity to once again "host the divine." Paul clearly disclosed the long-hidden mystery that Christ had come to reopen the door to Eden, leading us back into a place of eternal fellowship with God. And the possibility that every human being can be filled with the fullness of God through the sacrifice of the "second Adam" is, within itself, unspeakably glorious (1 Corinthians 15:22; Romans 5 & 6).

The stunning reality is that God's long journey to find a home on Earth has come to an end. When the "second Adam" (Christ) was put to sleep on the cross, the creation of the "second Eve" (the Church) began to take shape. Just as Eve was taken from the wound in Adam's side, the Church was formed from the pierced side of Jesus. At the exact moment that Jesus exhaled His last breath on Earth, the mystical Bride of Christ inhaled her original breath and began the divine commission to become a holy habitation of Christ.

Finally, the "Follow Me" statement makes sense. God has at last found a place to lay His head, and we who believe today are His Eve. Together with the "second Adam," we are the resting place of God. We are a collective house that reflects the extraordinary glory of the Creator.

Gateway to Heaven

Why have I taken the time to present this complex narrative of God's journey to find a home on Earth?

First and foremost, at the heart of this story is the mystery of the gospel unveiled. And to believe this marvelous story opens up a spiritual passageway that guides us back to the beginning or, more accurately, back to the future. Ultimately, this portal created by Christ leads us to our eternal abode in God—and His abode in us.

I'm honestly not sure how to describe it in words, except to say that the Lord has opened a door in the spirit realm, giving us access to His glory. It might sound strange, but the most nonreligious description I've ever heard came from a lady in North Carolina. She told me that en route to my conference, she had been "portalized"—caught up into an encounter with the supernatural.

At the moment, I admit that I was somewhat suspicious, thinking there was no such thing as being "portalized." For heaven's sake it wasn't even a real word. Regardless of my skepticism, however, the look on her face told me she had experienced something truly wonderful. She was beaming with excitement and dancing around the room like a little girl. Barely able to contain her enthusiasm, she began to blurt out the story of her encounter.

She explained how she had led a conservative life in a church that had little regard for the supernatural realm. Lately, however, she had begun to seek out a greater spiritual reality. On her way to the meeting, she made an amazing connection with the power of God and went through what she described as a spiritual gateway. All she knew was that something from Heaven reached out and touched her life.

"It was like the glory of God caught me up into a portal-like cloud," she said with great excitement. "I was portalized and everything around me began to spin around, swirling like a giant whirlwind."

Although I was happy for the woman, I left thinking that she was really sweet but a little odd. Then while driving home, I remembered that John had seen an open door in Revelation 4:1-3 and heard a voice beckoning him to a supernatural encounter with the Resurrected Christ:

"I looked and behold a door [portal] standing open in Heaven.... Immediately I was in the Spirit and behold a throne was standing in Heaven and One sitting on the throne. And He who was sitting was like a jasper stone and a sardius in appearance, and there was a rainbow around the throne like an emerald in appearance."

Then I remembered that Jacob also encountered a heavenly portal that greatly impacted his life. Genesis 28:12-16 declares that the heavens were opened in a dream, and he saw a ladder stretched from Heaven to Earth, with angels ascending and descending. Then from the top of the portal the Lord spoke to the patriarch about his purpose and destiny. When Jacob awoke, he uttered in amazement,

> "Surely the Lord is in this place and I did not know it." He was afraid and said, "How awesome is this place is! This is none other than the House of God, and this is the gate of Heaven."

At that point, I realized how important spiritual encounters can be to our quest for authentic existence today—even when we don't always know how to describe them. Of course, I'm reluctant to embrace manifestations of spiritual phenomena that are not God-centered. Nor do I want to oversimplify the "mystery of godliness" spoken about in Scripture. But like Jacob, John, and that lady in North Carolina, I believe that you and I are privileged to host the divine—to welcome God into our hearts.

At this very moment, we have a window of opportunity to connect with the Creator like no other time in history. With greater and greater intensity, God is coming in and out of this spiritual gateway, attempting to bond with His creation. And if we keep knocking on Heaven's door, one day He will come and stay forever. I'm not just speaking about us living in Heaven in the next life, but about God *living in us*—right here at this very moment in time.

Now that's Heaven on Earth!

Things to Consider

There is no appropriate way to end the inexhaustible subject about God living in man except to say that He is not the least bit appalled by our humanity. This Holy God who Scripture portrays as the "Ancient of Days" seems to be comfortable living in temples of flesh and blood. I'm not saying He is at home in all men, but those who are held captive by His embrace are privileged to accommodate His presence.

However, as I have contended throughout this book, many people are blind to the reality that their life is beyond ordinary. They struggle to produce miracles that will prove God's existence, when the biggest miracle before us is men and women made in His image. Knowing this, I often find myself staring deep into people's eyes, looking for a reflection of the Creator in their soul. My desire is to see the mystery of godliness that has been hidden in the heart of humanity since the beginning of creation.

> The human race is on a spiritual odyssey that will take us back to our future.

Perhaps there is a bit of impatience in me that is out of sync with God's eternal clock. I'm not sure, but I am convinced that the human race is on a spiritual odyssey that will take us back to our future. Even more amazing is the possibility that we can catch our original breath and recover the intimate relationship with the Creator that was choked out by the fall of Adam and Eve in the Garden of Eden.

When thinking of these things, I still go outdoors as I did when I was a boy and gaze at the brilliant display of distant galaxies. Not surprisingly, they continue to beckon me to a place in God that I could only imagine as a child. The only difference now is that I'm no longer looking to go somewhere. Instead, I am asking the Creator to come down and live big in houses of flesh that were created for His habitation.

When this comes to pass, our lives will be forever changed. As eternity fills our souls, we will be carried to the threshold of unbelievable destinies and breathe the very air of Heaven. In time, we will understand that life is not measured by the number of breaths we take, but by the moments that take our breath away.

"What is man that You take thought of him?
You have made him a little lower
than God, and You crown
him with glory and
majesty."
—Psalm 8:4-5—

Other Books by Larry Randolph

User Friendly Prophecy

The Coming Shift

Spirit Talk

Popular Audio Teachings by Larry Randolph

2010: Blue Moon Rising Conference

Spiritual Dynamics of the Word

Developing Your Prophetic Gift

The Humpty Dumpty Factor

The Coming Renaissance

Our Great Redemption

Discerning the Times

The Divine Embrace

The Face of God

For a complete list of resources, visit:

www.larryrandolph.com